FOOD
for all the
FAMILY

MAGNUS PYKE

FOOD
for all the
FAMILY

ILLUSTRATIONS BY BILL TIDY

JOHN MURRAY

ACKNOWLEDGEMENTS

Grateful acknowledgement is given
to Gerald Duckworth & Co Ltd
for permission to use an extract from
'The Python' from *More Beasts for Worse Children*
by Hilaire Belloc
and to Hutchinson Publishing Group Ltd
for permission to quote from 'Puddings'
from *All Pam's Poems* by Pam Ayres

AND THANKS

To Jean Macqueen for her kindly severity in pursuit
of accuracy – Dundee cake *is* better than Madeira
(and more British).
To Phyllis McDougall for her impeccable index, the ABC
and XYZ to adequate eating.
To Bill Tidy for his irreverent clutch at
– or should I say grasp of –
nutritional science.
M.P.

© Magnus Pyke 1980
Illustrations by Bill Tidy
© John Murray (Publishers) Ltd 1980

First published 1980 by
John Murray (Publishers) Ltd
50 Albemarle Street, London W1X 4BD

Printed and bound in Great Britain
at The Pitman Press, Bath

British Library Cataloguing in Publication Data
Pyke, Magnus
Food for all the family.
1. Nutrition
1. Title
641.1 TX551
ISBN 0-7195-3720-7

CONTENTS

1

2

3

4

ONE

Good Health

' . . . a lady who gave herself mercury poisoning by regularly eating
a pound or so of swordfish a day !'

THE FIRST THING to understand is that your nutrition is probably quite satisfactory already, provided that you are feeling fit and well and that you are neither too fat nor too thin. You really don't need a doctor or a nutritional scientist to tell you whether or not this is so. There is no need, therefore, to frighten yourself by worrying whether you have been poisoning or half-starving yourself for years. Almost certainly, you have been eating a reasonably sensible diet and there is no cause to make any change in it.

Yes, things really are as easy as this, in spite of all those muddling and sometimes misleading articles on nutrition that you may have been reading in magazines.

What to Eat to be Well Fed

You may have read that foods are composed of so-called 'nutrients' – protein, carbohydrate, fat, a list of twenty or so of minerals such as calcium, iron, copper, zinc, selenium, magnesium, iodine and manganese – as well as about as many vitamins. A great deal of confusion, doubt and nonsense has arisen in the public consciousness from all this well-meant information. The professional nutritionist needs to know all these details, just as the expert car designer needs to know how much chromium should be in the steel he is proposing to make his crankshaft out of. But this is of little interest to the owner-driver of a car.

PROTEIN

The ordinary owner-driver of a body gains very little useful guidance from a dissertation on protein because there is almost no way he (or she) could put together a diet providing enough to eat which did *not* supply as much, or more, protein as he needed. Protein turns up in almost every food, with two exceptions: there is no protein in sugar, and virtually none in fat (lard, butter, margarine or cooking oil). Since no one eats a diet made up of only sugar and fat, everyone who gets enough to eat – and that includes nearly everyone in western society – obtains his protein without any difficulty at all.

Scientists have a long history of muddled thinking when they try to give advice about protein and particularly about the merits of 'animal protein', which is derived from meat, chicken, fish, eggs, milk and cheese, compared with 'vegetable protein' which is derived from bread, potatoes and almost everything else. There are two main reasons for this. The first is that children in particular *do* thrive better if they get some animal protein: milk is the obvious way to give it to them. The second reason is that *people like meat*, and indeed it has a number of virtues. Just the same, facts can become confused with opinions. If you enjoy meat but cannot afford to buy as much as you would like, think of all the perfectly healthy vegetarians there are in the world, and of all those equally healthy people who do eat meat, milk, cheese and eggs but who eat much less of these foods than you do.

Please do not be misled. There must be protein in a good diet. If you were silly enough to try to do without it and to choose to live on cooking oil, sugar, boiled tapioca and gin, you would soon suffer nutritional disaster. But ordinary adults have *no need to worry* about the protein content of their food.

VITAMINS

Fifteen or twenty chemical compounds present in small amounts in a wide variety of food have come to be classified as 'vitamins'. The name arose when scientists were just beginning to find out about them. The process of discovery was exciting and the roles of the various vitamins in the operation of the processes of living were often unexpected.

But although all this was great fun for the scientists it was often misleading for ordinary people. For example, it is fascinating for a boxer to be aware that each time he delivers a left hook to his opponent's jaw, vitamin B_1 combined with phosphate has taken part in the breakdown of pyruvic acid derived from blood glucose in the release of the energy behind the punch; but he should not imagine that he would win more fights if he ate a slice of brown bread (which contains the vitamin) or swallowed a vitamin tablet between rounds.

The question remains: 'What does the ordinary person need to know about vitamins to ensure that he eats enough of them?' The answer is that there is very little need for grown-up people to bother about vitamins at all. *Too much has been written about vitamins*, and far too many claims have been made about what they can do for people who buy expensive foods that have been 'fortified' with this or that. As far as adults are concerned: *if you eat an ordinary mixture of ordinary wholesome food, you will obtain all the vitamins you need.*

This is because most of the vitamins are spread quite widely. Vitamin A, for example, occurs in butter and margarine, carrots, liver and kidneys, as well as in other foods. It follows, therefore, that you pick up the vitamin every day as you go along. And most of us carry about a year's supply inside our bodies – although people are not quite so expert as rats, which can store in their livers enough vitamin A to keep them going for a century, even though they live for only three or four years. The B-vitamins (there are half a dozen or more of these) are also found in all sorts of foods – in bread and beer, in milk and porridge, in liver and bacon, in peanuts and meat.

In short, as long as people ring the changes in choosing the things they eat in a sensible way, they will get all the vitamins they need. It is therefore a waste of time and money to go out and buy vitamin pills to eat. Although the name 'vitamins' sounds rather as though these substances could in some way 'vitalise' you, each vitamin is merely a chemical component of food that keeps your internal machinery running sweetly. If you are getting the amount you need, eating more is not going to do you any good. It certainly will not give you extra vigour or some kind of 'positive' health.

It is just as well, however, to keep an eye on the vitamin C in your diet. Nearly all living things make their own vitamin C in their bodies: only man and a few other animals cannot do so. (Those who, like us, need to eat the vitamin are rather an odd bunch: guinea pigs, fruit-eating bats, the red-vented bulbul bird from India, the apes and certain species of fish.) The ordinary citizen, however, needs to know only two things about vitamin C. The first is that *it occurs only in fruit and vegetables to any extent*, and the second is that *it is progressively destroyed if food is kept hot*. This is why home-cooked hot meals are often better than restaurant or hotel meals, or even – and this is sad – than 'meals on wheels'.

All this means that to make sure you get enough vitamin C you should see to it each week that some of your meals include freshly cooked potatoes and greens, or that you have had some fresh fruit. There is good sense in the saying 'an apple a day keeps the doctor away'.

People often talk, quite rightly, about the desirability of eating at least 'one good cooked meal' a day. This is mainly because most people depend on the potatoes and greens in this 'one good cooked meal' for their vitamin C. When they put emphasis on it being a 'good' cooked meal they are implying that the gravy has not been dried up on the plate nor are the greens and potatoes shrivelled and tired by having been kept hot in the oven waiting for father to come home while mother is out playing bingo.

The other vitamins are of little practical interest to ordinary people. Much of the information so con- scientiously disseminated about them therefore does no good and, particularly if it helps to make people faddy, can actually do harm. Signs and symptoms of shortage of any of the four or five components of what once used to be called 'vitamin B' *are virtually never seen* in western societies. Beriberi can strike down prisoners of war held in labour camps in the tropics and may occur in poor communities living mainly on polished rice. Pellagra was once a scourge among poverty-stricken French and Spanish peasants who lived chiefly on maize meal and among the wretchedly poor farm-workers in the southern United States. But beriberi and pellagra are unknown today in industrialised countries. It follows that all those B-vitamins listed on the cornflakes packets are of little significance to the sort of people who eat cornflakes.

Vitamin A has interested scientists for years and it can be fascinating to hear them talk about its function in the mechanism by which, after stumbling from bright sunshine into a darkened cinema you can in a moment or two find an empty seat and avoid the embarrassment of sitting down on somebody's lap in one already occupied. It is true that your eyes become adapted to the dim light by a complex process in which vitamin A plays a part. But it would be difficult to the verge of impossibility to identify a single individual whose eyes cannot adapt to a dim light because he has eaten too little vitamin A. This is because there is vitamin A in butter and, in properly run communities, it is put into margarine during the course of its manufacture. There is vitamin A in cheese and its equivalent in greens and carrots. And even if you do not eat butter or margarine or carrots and greens or – as many, perhaps, do not – herring or liver, you have no cause to worry because just as the cod stores huge amounts of vitamin A in its liver (hence the richness in vitamins of cod-liver oil) so also do you. However frugally you live as a rule, a good blow-out on your birthday, or a feast at Christmas, could provide enough vitamin A to keep you in the vitamin for six months.

Children need vitamin D to protect them from rickets

but grown-up people are exceedingly unlikely to suffer from its lack. And most of the other vitamins are of little more than specialist interest even to scientists; so they are as unimportant to the average eater as would be a debate on the wax content of shoe polish. This practical insignificance associated with the publication of bizarre experimental results emanating from research laboratories has led unfortunately to a flood of unconfirmed nonsense descending on the innocent heads of ordinary people who only want to know what nutrition is all about. Vitamin E, for example, has been claimed to protect people against all sorts of complaints from ill temper to sterility. In fact, there is not only no evidence that any ordinary diet is ever deficient in vitamin E but it is doubtful whether human beings (as distinct from rats or chickens) have any need for vitamin E in their food at all.

When vitamins are important. Nothing in all this should be taken as casting any slur on the great amount of study and discovery contributed by gifted scientists and physicians as far back as the 18th century, but mainly during the last eighty years or so. Scientists now understand in detail the chemistry of the various forms in which vitamin A can exist, its role in the functioning of the eye and something – but not, so far, all – of its part in the growth and well-being of animals and men. They now know not only that vitamin B_1 is necessary for the prevention of a specific deficiency disease, but they also understand how it operates at one particular stage in the release of the energy needed by every living creature. Similar quite detailed understanding of several other B-vitamins is available. Much, too, has been done to elucidate the functioning of the different chemical forms of vitamin D in maintaining the healthy structure of bone.

It is important for physicians, who specialise in these things, to understand the latest observations in biochemistry, and we can take pride in the government's advisers insisting on the addition of vitamins to white bread and margarine. Those responsible for the well-being of communities living in the quite different circumstances of Africa or Asia must also be well informed about the whole range of nutritional knowledge. Nevertheless, the ordinary citizen of a western industrial community, anxious to ensure for himself a good and healthy diet, can easily become confused or misled by this plethora of information that is irrelevant and inapplicable to his own nutrition.

Minerals

A loose but nevertheless reasonably scientific definition of food is 'something that keeps you going'. Suppose that you are lost in the jungle, and you come across some honey in a wild bees' nest; quite rightly, you gasp out 'food'. A dead rat, a crumb of chocolate in the bottom of a knapsack, even an old boot, carefully boiled as it was by Charlie Chaplin in *The Gold Rush*, is rightly recognised as food. And all these fit into the definition. At its most basic and elementary level, food *is* something that keeps you going. Nevertheless the definition can only be described as loosely scientific. For example, *salt* does not exactly keep you going, yet it is an essential part of a proper diet. Where salt is scarce people (and animals too) know that they need it. Indeed, they lust after it and their governments, following the way of governments everywhere discovering something that people like very much (it is drink and tobacco with us), have been known to put a tax on salt.

Salt is one of a whole group of substances which are necessary for a good diet, and which are commonly lumped together under the general title of 'minerals'. It is a good example of the group. People are well aware that they need it. At the same time, since it is usually readily available they do not if they are sensible worry about it. It is cheap, plentiful, turns up naturally in a variety of common foods –

for example, bread, butter and kippers – and can be taken or left alone according to taste without doing a body any particular good or harm.

Calcium is another mineral to which public attention is drawn from time to time. Just like the vitamins, it is essential to health. Again, however, most grown people get all they want merely by eating. Calcium, which is the main component of chalk and marble, goes into the structure of bones; this means that children, whose bones are growing, need much more calcium, and need it more urgently, than do adults, whose bones are fully grown. But it is doubtful whether old people, who can so easily break a thigh bone in a trivial fall off the kerb, can prevent their skeletons from becoming fragile by eating extra calcium in their food. So once again it seems reasonable for the ordinary grown-up citizen not to bother about calcium. Cheese is good food, to be sure, but it is more sensible to eat it because you like it than because of the calcium it supplies. After all, it would be a shame to spend good money on cheese that you did not happen to like, just because of its calcium, if you were already eating enough calcium anyway.

Iron is a different matter. It forms part of the red pigment of blood, and red blood is a good thing to have. Anaemia, the lack of this red pigment, is the commonest of all nutritional defects. Indeed, it is often the *only* sign of nutritional deficiency the public-health authorities ever find. Always, it is commonest among women, because of their monthly loss of blood in the menstrual discharge. Men are not immune, and those who suffer regular bleeding from piles may similarly become anaemic. Curiously enough, although the importance of iron in food has been known for a long time and although iron is not difficult to detect and measure, we still do not completely understand the best way to obtain it and exactly how to make the body take up what it wants. It was once fashionable to pooh-pooh the old-time 'tonics', which were mostly mixtures of iron salts, but they may well turn out to have been useful after all. It has, at last, been recognised by the *cognoscenti* that your grandmother's iron cooking pots were indeed useful and that the rust and tang they contributed to grandfather's food actually did him good!

Iodine is customarily grouped with the minerals, and it is one which everyone needs. In some parts of the world it is common to see people with a characteristic swelling of the neck, called goitre, which develops when they do not get enough iodine in their food. Iodine occurs in tiny amounts in sea-water, and also in fish. In most parts of a sea-girt island like Great Britain, iodine is blown on to the soil in the sea-spray, and is taken up by the plants and animals raised there, so that most of the population's needs are met. This is not invariably so, however; goitre was at one time common in Derbyshire – it was once known as 'Derbyshire neck'. But I am not suggesting that housewives who live in places where goitre is common should season the gravy with a teaspoonful of tincture of iodine (the form in which a chemist usually sells iodine). This would be far too much: the amount you need is exceedingly small. It is much better to insist that the public-health authorities see to it that the salt sold in the local supermarkets is laced with small quantities of iodine.

Even though goitre is now rare and most people have no need to worry about whether their food contains enough iodine, yet this is one of the minerals that it is useful to know something about. Traditionally, most of the British ate plenty of iodine because of the ready availability of fish from the sea. Today, however, the price of fish has soared – fish and chips have already almost become a luxury – and perhaps the situation may change. And the consequences of a serious iodine shortage could be grave. In parts of the highlands of Peru, for instance, stunted people with serious mental deficiency are often encountered. They are called cretins; and the cause of their disability is a lack of iodine from birth.

There are other minerals that have to be obtained from

food. But again, the actual amounts required each day are exceedingly small, and ordinary people virtually never go short of any of these. Things may be different for growing children, or for people in distant and deprived parts of the world. Unless you happen to like the taste and have money to waste, there is no rational justification for your buying mineral tablets purporting to supply copper, vanadium, zinc or selenium. Undoubtedly, if with immense trouble almost all the copper is removed from a rat's food, the rat in due course becomes anaemic. But unless you are an experimental rat, not only will you obtain your needs of copper from your ordinary meals but it is almost impossible for you not to. Furthermore, there is a chance that you might actually poison yourself with too much copper and make yourself ill. The necessity for selenium in the diet has not been recognised for very long, but the amounts needed are minute. Long before the need for selenium was established, however, it was recognised as being highly poisonous – more poisonous than arsenic. In parts of the United States where the soil is comparatively rich in selenium, livestock die if allowed to graze on certain pastures because of the high selenium levels in the grasses there. And selenium is just one example of an element that is essential in tiny quantities but poisonous if you eat too much. So a certain amount of caution is advisable.

Besides the minerals that you *do* need and which, except under extraordinary circumstances, you get anyway and therefore need not worry about, there are others that turn up in foods and that you do *not* need. *Cadmium*, for instance, turns up in minute quantities in all kinds of foods. It is used in the electroplating industry but it is also present in traces in certain plastics and sometimes in the pigments used to decorate cooking vessels. You can probably consume about half a milligram a week of cadmium without coming to any harm. In Great Britain a week's food contains about a fifth of a milligram on average, so that most ordinary citizens do not consume enough cadmium to bother about. The only way you might conceivably come to harm (unless, of course, you are an electroplater involved in an accident) is to live almost exclusively on crabmeat! Although no one understands why, crabs possess a special proclivity for accumulating cadmium out of the water they live in, even when the amount in the water is very little indeed.

Lead, too, lies all around us and gets into all sorts of food and drink whether we like it or not. At one time canned food contained more than it should, but the levels were made safe by changing the way in which the cans were soldered. When water pipes were all made of lead and plumbers really were plumbers (the word means a worker in lead), people could be poisoned by their own drinking water, particularly if the water was soft.

You can probably consume up to three milligrams a week of lead without coming to any harm. Since the latest estimates indicate that a week's consumption of British food contains about one and a quarter milligrams, you are unlikely to get lead poisoning from your food.

Some years ago a number of Japanese fishermen and their families died of what was later discovered to be *mercury* poisoning. This was because a factory nearby was discharging mercury into Minimata Bay. The mercury was changed by the micro-organisms in the water into methylmercury, which is very poisonous indeed. In due course the methylmercury was consumed by the fish and the fish by the fishermen, who lived very largely on their own catch. When this became known, of course, a tremendous hubbub arose, the public-health authorities everywhere began to analyse fish and – regardless of the fact that they had been eating fish all their lives without dying – some people became frightened. In the United States mercury was detected in canned tuna fish, and almost everyone became afraid to eat it. Later, it emerged that even those tuna fish living in the purest and most uncontaminated waters had a small amount of mercury in their flesh. Mercury was actually found in a preserved tuna that had been put into a museum long before factories existed in the United States. And tuna are not alone; cod and other deep-sea fish also have some mercury in them. It now appears, firstly, that everyone who eats fish is bound to consume some mercury, be it ever so little. Secondly, it is generally agreed that 0.3 milligrams of mercury a week, of which not more than 0.2 milligrams is in the form of methylmercury, is probably harmless. All the same, it is a good thing to be sensible, and factories that use mercury in their processes should be kept under good control and not allowed to release their effluents into the sea, particularly in a bay or enclosed waterway. It is also sensible for you not to restrict your diet to a single kind of food no matter how much you fancy it. An American scientific journal reported the peculiar case of a lady who gave herself mercury poisoning by regularly eating a pound or so of swordfish a day!

FAT

Fat is good to eat, although you shouldn't eat too much of it. There has been so much talk about the harmful effects of fat in the newspapers and on television that some people have got a biased view of the whole business. Anyone who has forgotten to do the shopping and tries to make a meal of dry bread soon finds out that bread and butter is better to eat. Everyone knows, too, that fried potatoes form an agreeable alternative to plain mash now and then, and that a lump of butter can improve the plain mashed potatoes as well.

The principal disadvantages of fat arise from its remarkably high fuel value. It contains more than twice as many calories as sugar or flour. (A calorie is simply a measure of the energy-value of food. More commonly nowadays a larger unit, the Calorie, which is the equivalent of 1,000 calories, is used. See Units, p.250.) Moreover, the fat on meat and cooking fat and lard do not contain water, or at most very little – while such foods as bread, potatoes and all the ordinary cooked dishes contain quite large amounts. All this implies that a mouthful of fat contributes a large amount of food value. If, therefore you eat fat, not just because you are hungry but because you like its taste and texture, and do so day after day, there is a good chance that you will become fat. And fatness – obesity, as it is more precisely termed – is the commonest kind of malnutrition to be found in prosperous communities.

Too much fat, especially the fat of meat, butter and cream, has also been implicated in heart attacks, particularly among middle-aged men. I shall talk about eating to avoid obesity and – as far as possible – heart disease, in later chapters.

STARCH

In *Alice Through the Looking Glass*, the White King remarks:

'There is nothing like a ham sandwich when you're feeling faint.'

'I should have thought a little sal volatile would have been better,' replied Alice, in her common-sense way.

'I didn't say there was nothing better,' said the King. 'I said there was nothing like it.'

The White King, in his wisdom, knew that when you are hungry, bread is an excellent food. And the main component of bread (not the *only* component, but the main one) is starch. In other parts of the world, rice is an alternative vehicle for starch. Likewise starch is the principal ingredient (apart from water) in potatoes, and also in maize products such as cornflour and breakfast cereals.

Now starch has a particular nutritional function: to contribute energy-value to the diet – in other words, to keep you going when you are hungry. This is a most important function. A great deal of attention is nowadays devoted to the problems of obesity, which are only of significance to people who eat too much; but we must not forget that when times are hard (and for that matter in ordinary times as well) bread is still the 'staff of life', mainly because of the starch in it.

Of course, protein and fat supply energy-value too. When you are hungry and settle down to eat a plateful of bacon and eggs, you are satisfying your hunger on the protein and fat of which they are mainly composed. On the other hand, when you eat bread, rice pudding, pie crust, biscuits or potatoes, it is the starch in them that for the most part takes the edge off your appetite. In cake, or in a helping of roast beef and Yorkshire pudding or a bag of fish and chips, or in a sausage roll all three ingredients – fat, protein and starch – make their joint contribution.

SUGAR

It is worth discussing sugar at some length because, of all articles of diet, sugar has been made the target of some of the most misleading and nonsensical statements masquerading as 'nutritional education'.

The first thing to be said is that sugar has an agreeable taste – and there is no harm in that! Secondly, it is useful in cooking; without sugar good cakes would be hard to make, and jam (surely one of the modest pleasures of life) would disappear. Thirdly, sugar contributes energy-value to the diet; a pound of sugar contains 12 per cent more energy-value than a pound of flour.

But as well as having these three good qualities sugar can be accused of three bad things: one for what it does *not* do and two for what it does. Firstly, sugar is *only* carbohydrate. That is to say, it is not a mixture of carbohydrate, protein, vitamins and a few other things, as bread is. So if people are unwise enough to eat too high a proportion of sugar in their diet, they may go short of protein, vitamins or minerals. But this is no justification for telling the rest of us, who have more sense, that white sugar is a 'poison'. It is not. Secondly, sugar is so concentrated a source of energy-value that it is easy to eat so much of it in syrup sponge, iced cakes and over-sweetened tea, and so become fat. The third bad feature of sugar is that too much of it, and especially frequent sucking of sticky sweets, can cause your teeth to decay. Decayed teeth are more prevalent in the world's best-fed populations and among those with the greatest amount of sugar in their diets; the best preventative measures that we have are not particularly effective and the cost of the repair and replacement of the nation's damaged teeth is enormous.

All that being said, there is still no scientific reason to stop people who like cake and jam and even sweet tea from eating with a clear conscience a very useful and agreeable commodity – but *in moderation*.

ROUGHAGE

Roughage is a popular topic of conversation among people who take an interest in their health and what they eat. Sometimes the particular attention which they give to the activity of their bowels could be described as positively *unhealthy*. Fortunes have been made by the distributors of laxative pills claimed to be worth 'a guinea a box', and by the purveyors of powders guaranteed to ensure 'inner cleanliness', whatever that is supposed to be. Those who believe in the nutritional virtues of roughage need to assess carefully the known hard facts if they are to escape the charge of worshipping the 'Bowel Movement' as an article of faith.

The *facts* appear to be as follows:

☐ Roughage, which can loosely be defined as mainly indigestible fibrous material in food, makes a small contribution to the energy-value of the diet but there is little evidence that it adds significantly to the nutritional value of what is eaten.

☐ There is some doubt as to exactly what 'roughage' is. The bran and husks in wholemeal flour appear to have a different composition from that of the fibrous material in, say, cabbage stalks, which can also be described as roughage.

☐ It is sometimes argued that African tribes whose members eat a coarse diet with much more roughage in it than westerners are accustomed to suffer far less from 'diseases of civilisation', whatever those are supposed to be. Recent studies have shown, however, that African tribesmen have fewer doctors than we do to tell them whether they are ill or not and themselves suffer from diseases which westerners never see.

☐ There is some reason to believe that a certain condition of the bowel, called diverticulosis, may be less common among those who eat a lot of roughage. People can have this condition without knowing it but sometimes it does become troublesome. Some doctors also believe that cancer of the bowel is commoner among those whose diet contains less fibre than it is among those who eat a good deal. The problem is to know whether a normal diet contains enough – or too much – roughage. There is other experimental evidence, equally strong, suggesting that too much fibre can blot up useful ingredients of the diet as they pass through the digestive system.

Although one day someone may be able to show that people *are* healthier when they go out of their way to eat extra roughage, the present situation seems to be that people eat wholemeal bread, branny breakfast cereals and cabbage stalks (if anyone does eat cabbage stalks) because they like them and because they *believe* that a diet with a lot of roughage in it does them good, rather than because there is much evidence to show that this is so. There is certainly no convincing reason for the claims made by the super-enthusiasts that roughage is the only sure passport to physical well-being. It seems to me to be sensible to steer a middle course until more scientific knowledge comes to light and is proved in practice to be useful. A healthy person who eats sensibly and lives a reasonable life, taking enough exercise to keep fit, has little need to bother himself about his bowels.

Simple Rules for Good Nutrition

In spite of the clamour of advice from 'experts', faddists and enthusiasts for honey, wholemeal bread, black treacle and laxatives, it is easy for any sensible man or woman – and not very much more difficult for an intelligent child (or its mother) – to choose a nourishing diet. And if your diet provides the nourishment your body needs, then no further benefit, no super-health, no dynamic virility (or femininity) or magical protection against colds or flu, will be gained by eating extra amounts of one thing or drinking extra quantities of another.

There are really just two rules for good nutrition:

☐ *Have enough to eat.* This means that most people should be able to eat until they are no longer hungry. Unlucky people who tend to get fat if they do this must find a way to finish eating while they are still hungry.

☐ *Eat a good mixture of foods.* While there is no need to fuss too much about individual meals, it is a good idea to make sure that by the end of the day you have eaten a mixture of different kinds of food. And there is good nutritional sense, as well as fun, in changing your diet on a Sunday or at Christmas or when Lent is over. It is also good practice to change the selection of foods as the seasons change. This is perhaps even more important now that manufactured foods – good though they may be – are inevitably uniform in their composition. Keep in mind in particular three kinds of food, and include each group in your daily mixture if you can:

(*a*) Cereals and the foods made from them are all useful. But man cannot live on bread alone – or even on bread, rice, tapioca, semolina and cornflakes. Butter, margarine and dripping make bread more satisfying. Nevertheless even a diet made up of bread and butter or pastry would be nutritionally unsatisfactory.

(*b*) The occasional egg (either as such or mixed in a cake or pudding), a piece of cheese, a little milk, and meat and fish all usefully complement bread and cereals. It is not essential to eat meat and fish, but it is easier to be well nourished if you do.

(*c*) The White King's favourite ham sandwiches are nourishing and filling; but think how you would feel if you had to live for a long time on *nothing* else. Potatoes, greens, fruit, orange juice, carrots, turnips, lettuce and tomato – these round off the mixture.

It is easy to see from these rules why cooked meals can constitute a good diet more easily than sandwiches and snacks. The main course brings in meat or fish, perhaps with cereals if the meat is made up into sausages or a pie. Best of all, potatoes and greens fit in more 'naturally' than does, for example, a slice of tomato or a lettuce leaf which may *not* be part of a sandwich. Apple pie or fruit salad and cream – mixtures of foods from groups (*a*) and (*c*) – diversify cooked meals, whereas cold-snack-eaters may not trouble to eat fruit as well.

But although a cooked meal eaten each day in among the others makes it easier to consume a mixture of bread-and-butter-type foods, meat-milk-and-egg-type foods and fruit and vegetables (whether fresh or frozen doesn't matter), it is not essential to health to eat hot food. A person could live out his days on some of the 'club sandwiches' that are served in the United States. And many snack lunches made up from sandwiches, a piece of cake, an apple or an orange and a flask of tea, provide an admirable balance of nutrients.

People sometimes seem to lose their sense of reality when they start worrying about good nutrition and begin to fuss about every mouthful, let alone each meal. You know quite well that you can miss a meal – and food that is not there to be eaten is obviously lacking in *every* nutrient – without coming to any harm. If you get stuck on a mountain you can go without food for a whole day without damaging your health. Enough to eat and the proper food to choose are matters that are important in the general pattern of living, not in hour-by-hour detail. Perhaps, after having grasped the simple directions for putting together a good diet, the next rule of nutrition for you to learn is '*don't fuss*'.

This rule of nutrition is easy for most of us to follow. But all of us make things more difficult for ourselves to some extent by deliberately labelling some perfectly wholesome articles of food as uneatable. Nearly everybody, for instance, rejects the practice of cannibalism even though, as far as I know, human flesh represents a tasty and nutritious food resource. And most of us would probably decline a plateful of fried earthworms or a bowl of caterpillar soup. Taboos like these are deep-rooted, dating back to the dawn of our history, and are only discarded under the most extreme pressures of starvation – frequently not even then. Moreover, some foods are regarded as inedible by certain races or groups even though other people relish them thoroughly: if you are a Jew or a Muslim, for example, you will not touch pork, for instance, or if you're a Hindu, beef. Many people refuse to eat meat of any kind at all, and there are even some who will not touch dairy produce either.

Now if you are among those who choose their food fairly freely, you have no problems here. If you jib at just a few delicacies such as tripe or pigs' ears for some fancied aesthetic reason or other, you won't have much difficulty either. But if you severely restrict your diet by choosing to regard a great many different foods as unacceptable – however high-minded your reasons – you make it very hard for yourself to follow the second rule for good nutrition. For example, you will get plenty of iron in your diet if you eat meat several times a week. If you decide to become a strict vegetarian, however, you will have to take care that you get the iron you need from some other foods. You could make sure of your iron supplies by including dried fruit, chocolate and black treacle in the mixture you select. You may fear that eating chocolate and treacle will make you fat, and that you have to begin helping yourself very sparingly to other sugary foods: but after all, that is a dilemma that you have created for yourself by deciding not to eat meat, isn't it?

Keeping Fit

'. . . you ought not to eat a huge meal just before swimming
300 metres freestyle . . .'

WE ARE ALL DIFFERENT: different in height and build, different in personality. But all of us know what we mean when we say we are 'fit'. A fit man, whatever his age, gets up in the morning feeling fresh and energetic, ready to relish whatever the day may bring; though by the evening he may be sleepy, his weariness is the healthy result of a day crammed with all kinds of activities, and will disappear after a good night's sleep. He does not share the dragging step, the ever-present 'below par' feeling, the trivial ailments – headaches, ill-defined twinges, chronic sniffles, persistent tiredness – that are all too familiar.

I am sure that you have, at least sometimes, shared this feeling of sparkling vigour. And you know that it certainly does not depend on what cereals you eat for breakfast, nor what bedtime drinks you choose. It does depend to some extent on your frame of mind and on the circumstances of your life. And quite often, the time when you are feeling at your peak of fitness is the time when you have recently shed a few surplus pounds: literally, when your step is at its lightest. Too many of us are just a little too heavy most of the time: but a fit person is at his or her ideal weight. It follows, therefore, that the fit person is eating just the right amount of food.

Many people can keep to their ideal weight from their early twenties right up to middle age without giving the matter a thought. And they do this even though they might take on a job requiring heavy physical labour and so eat more – because, of course, they need more then – and later on go back to less demanding work and eat less. For all those lucky people their appetite indicates their needs with remarkable accuracy. There are, however, others who possess a good appetite and like their food but whose appetite 'switches off' just a little bit too late. This means that they tend at each meal to eat a little more than they need, so that they put on weight. These people soon learn that they need to guard against eating too much food if they want to keep fit.

All Foods are Fattening Foods

Any food is fattening to the person who eats more of it than his body needs. The body takes the energy-value it needs and stores away the rest; and the clearest indication of overweight is this surplus energy-value, laid down as fat all over the body, but perhaps most conspicuously around the waistline, neck, hips and thighs.

☐ *The least fattening foods* are those with the most water in them. Fresh vegetables, for example, are mostly water. Indeed, a turnip is more of a drink than a food and contains more water than many beverages.

☐*Foods of intermediate fattening power* are also those that are fairly wet. Lean meat and gravy, for example, aren't very fattening. Nor are boiled potatoes provided you don't eat too much of them. Bread and foods made from flour obviously contribute energy-value so that if you eat a roll you do not really want you are taking aboard unnecessary fattening power. Cake is worse because it usually contains quite a lot of sugar (more fattening than flour) and fat.

☐*Really fattening foods* (it is so obvious) are foods which *are fat* or which *contain fat*. For instance, suet pudding is made of fat (and sugar and flour), meat fat is nearly all fat, *chipped* potatoes and *fried* fish are cooked in fat, and a lot of the fat clings to them. Cake and pastry have fat in them. Chocolate is mostly cocoa, butter as well as sugar. Anyone can make his own list, without help from me.

☐*Beer*, although it is wet, is a food. And beer is one of the commonest causes of obesity among people who like it. A pint of beer contains 200 calories, about the same as two slices of bread (a pint of stout contains nearer 300). If, therefore, a man eats all the food he needs during the day and then after his evening meal he strolls down the road and drinks five pints of beer (which can easily happen, can it not?) he is taking in 1,000 calories that he does not need. If his total daily requirement is about 2,500 calories, he is consuming 40 per cent more energy-value than he can use. No wonder he puts on weight.

Keeping Weight Down

DON'T EAT MORE THAN YOU NEED

In our wealthy modern society more is written about losing weight than about any other nutritional topic. The basic rules of dieting to this end are absurdly simple, but like the equally simple golden rule of good behaviour, they are difficult to keep. In order to lose weight, all you have to do is *eat less than you want to eat* and – probably for the rest of your life – *rise from the table* while you are still hungry.

It is because this, while easy to remember, is so difficult to do that there are dozens of different dietary formulas and hundreds of different 'slimming' systems, each guaranteed to do the trick better than the last. Sensible and reasonably strong-minded people will choose whichever of these regimes they find suits them best and will do their utmost to stick to it. If they persist, they may become accustomed to the smaller meals, or to meals lacking in fat, cake, chips, lumps of sugar and mayonnaise. They may cease to miss the evening pint (or perhaps the second pint they once would have drunk). It is wonderful what one can become used to.

If you are trying to lose weight or, at least, not to become any fatter, there are two kinds of food which you should avoid. The first kind are those foods which are concentrated sources of energy, which means they are rich in fat or low in moisture (for example, a spoonful of sugar contains almost no moisture and when put into a cup of tea or a cake adds nothing to its bulk, so that you hardly know you have eaten it. Secondly, it is wise to avoid those foods that are taken outside your regular meals. A chocolate or two, biscuits with the morning tea, a roll eaten casually while waiting for a meal to be served and, as damaging as any, a gin (containing the best part of the energy-value in half a pint of beer) or a night out with the boys – all these can undo days of self-restraint and rising unsatisfied from the table for those whose dishonest stomachs fail to tell them that they have eaten enough until after they have already eaten that little bit too much.

On the other hand, bulky but unsubstantial foods such as shredded raw cabbage or some of the filling vegetable dishes served in Chinese restaurants can fill the stomach, even though their energy-value is quite small.

YOUR FRAME OF MIND

Clubs for slimmers are an excellent idea because they provide opportunities for people to share their experiences of struggling to inure themselves to a lifetime of self-restraint, and to denying themselves the very real pleasure of eating as much as they can of foods that they like. Together they can steel themselves to their ordeal, revel in the readings of the bathroom scales which reward them for sticking to their resolve, and for very shame of what others of the group would think if they transgressed, resist moments of temptation. If left to themselves, of course, they would argue that one or two tiny little chocolate biscuits, or one evening out at the wife's sister's (whose cooking is so transcendental), would not do any harm.

The effectiveness of these 'Weight Watchers' and similar clubs in helping people with a tendency to corpulence illustrates the importance of your frame of mind, that is your determination, on your nutritional state. People tend to over-eat when they are worried or frustrated, and indeed obesity is most common among comparatively poor and unfortunate people. On the other hand, if you are busy with your hobbies or actively concerned in running your trade union or your Rotary Club or Townswomen's Guild, or vigorously organising a conference or a raffle, you are less likely to spend a lot of time over-eating – or, come to that, worrying about your figure.

KEEP MOVING!

Most people know that to keep fit they must take exercise. It does not matter whether you get it from a systematic course of physical training or from walking to work and walking home again, or even from the daily demands of work and domestic life. Though most people enjoy some particular sport or game, you can be perfectly fit from your ordinary daily activities even if you do not participate in sport at all.

Since food provides the fuel for the bodily engine, the amount of food that is needed is obviously related to the amount of work the engine does. After a day's walking in the hills it is natural and reasonable for you to feel hungry. You will have used up more fuel than you would have done at work if you normally work sitting down, either in front of a desk or on a fork-lift truck. Nevertheless, although most people can automatically adjust themselves to variations in the amount of exercise they take and so keep their weight reasonably steady for years on end, if you have an unlucky tendency to obesity you must still guard against fully satisfying your appetite even when strenuous activity has made you hungry.

Regular daily exercise is good nutritional practice for everyone, whether they are inclined to put on weight or not. The reason is that if you lead an almost entirely sedentary life, so that your need for food energy is low, the mechanism which balances your appetite against your physical needs becomes less accurate. Common-sense knowledge is scientifically true: it really is virtually impossible to keep fit without taking exercise. It is also very much harder not to gain weight.

The Thyroid in Control

The thyroid gland is a gland in your neck, and its particular function is to exercise control (almost like the accelerator pedal in a motor car) over the speed at which your internal machinery operates. Lively, bustling, animated people burn up more fuel merely existing over, say, an hour than people whose systems operate more slowly. It follows, therefore, that the individual with a high 'metabolic rate', as it is called, will need more food to keep going than someone who burns up fuel less quickly. Conversely, if these two people eat the same meals, the one with the slower metabolic rate will be more likely to get fat. And the metabolic rate depends on the activity of the thyroid.

To operate properly, the thyroid gland needs iodine, and people who do not eat enough iodine may develop goitre; their rate of metabolism may slow down and unless they eat less they will begin to put on weight. There are, however, other ways in which the thyroid gland can go wrong. If, therefore, a person suddenly finds himself unaccountably becoming lethargic and putting on weight, it may be because his thyroid has developed a defect, and is functioning too slowly. A person whose thyroid has become *over*-active, on the other hand, becomes tense and loses weight, and his eyes may begin to bulge. Both conditions respond well to medical treatment as a rule.

Food for Champions

People who set great store on success in games or sports often wonder whether some special diet would help them to run or swim faster, jump higher or hit a ball or another person harder. But provided that you have been accustomed to eating in the common-sense way I have been describing, the science of nutrition can do very little to help you win races, overcome at boxing or tennis, or become a champion swimmer. Here you are on your own. Nutrition can do only three things for you (and you can do these just as well for yourself):

☐ You must eat a sensible mixture like anyone else and not take up some faddy system that someone tells you they use in Outer Mongolia.

☐ If you are taking a lot of exercise, you must eat enough food to supply the extra energy-value you need. In order that this does not involve your sitting down to enormous bulky meals, you *do* require fat (on your steak or in your pudding) to provide the calories, bearing in mind that fat contributes more than twice as many calories as any other food ingredient.

☐ What an athlete eats must suit his digestion. This means you ought not to eat a huge meal just before swimming 300 metres freestyle nor fill yourself up with treacle tart before a football match if treacle tart gives you heartburn. But this is not science – it is common horse-sense.

Coaches, trainers and athletes themselves can often be heard praising one kind of diet or another. Some swear by vitamin tablets, and others put their trust in pints of milk or pounds of steak. In the Olympic village people can be heard praising jugs of orange juice or even glasses of stout. But all this has little to do with athletic excellence. There have been successful competitors who were vegetarians and others who ate a lot of meat. If you collect a hundred athletes together, all equally well fed and all equally able, well trained and practised, the one who wins is the one who is most determined to win. Fighting spirit, determination, stubbornness, confidence and courage rank high in successful sportsmen but have little to do with diet. On the other hand, a resourceful coach can put heart into a despondent sportsman by giving him a special drink or a pink pill if he can make the sportsman *believe* that it will do him good.

GLUCOSE

Some years ago, there was a murderer who chopped up his victims, stewed their remains in acid and then disposed of them by pouring them down the drain. What we all do to our meat and bread and other foods when we digest them is similar in principle to what the murderer did, though very much cleverer. Of course, instead of pouring the digested liquid food away, we absorb the food ingredients into our bloodstream through the partly porous walls of our digestive system. Part of the absorbed ingredients (one of which is glucose) is used as the current fuel supply to keep us going but most is stored away here and there around our bodies and is available for use whenever it may be required. Everyone knows that we don't run out of fuel every time we miss a meal, like a car with an empty petrol tank. In fact, the level of glucose in most people's blood almost always remains remarkably steady. Athletes, such as marathon runners, however, who exert enormous effort for a prolonged period of time, can use up so much fuel that they cannot release stored glucose from their tissues quickly enough to maintain a normal level in their blood. Their performance may be improved and their total exhaustion prevented if they take glucose tablets. Lumps of sugar would be almost as good. Ordinary people, however, will not find themselves miraculously energetic and lively if they take glucose; they are more likely to put on weight.

SALT

Salt is an essential ingredient of a good diet, but most

people living in industrialised societies obtain all the salt they need without having to worry about it, and people sprinkle salt on their food at table because they enjoy the taste, rather than because they need it as a nutrient. Athletes, however, may require extra salt if they are called upon to exert themselves for prolonged periods when the temperature and humidity are high. Long-distance runners, for instance, performing in hot weather may sweat so much, and lose so much salt in their sweat, that their bodies become deprived of salt, and this can lead to muscle cramp and even to exhaustion and collapse. This can equally affect workmen in foundries, in the engine-rooms of ships in tropical waters or in deep, hot mines.

The remedy for salt depletion is to take salt tablets, to eat salty food or even to drink beer to which salt has been added. If there really is a dietary need for salt – that is, if there has been considerable and prolonged sweating – salty beer will be found remarkably refreshing!

Is It Safe To Eat?

Some people worry far too much. Others don't worry enough.

White bread, white sugar, tinned vegetables, candy bars – at one time or another it has been fashionable to worry about all these things, even though in themselves they are perfectly harmless.

But on the other hand, there are aspects of nutritional science that are scarcely mentioned in public except with noses wrinkled in fastidious distaste – and yet that can be actually lethal.

'CHEMICALS' AND 'ADDITIVES'

A great deal of concern has been expressed, sometimes vociferously, about the presence of so-called 'additives' in foods. But just what are these 'additives'? Bakers add salt to bread, and bread without salt is rather unpleasant; but salt, or sodium chloride, can certainly be described as a 'chemical'. In making a birthday cake, a mother will colour the different layers of sponge pink or green or yellow – and the icing as well. Are the colours 'additives'? Like bakers, the food manufacturers add certain special-purpose materials to foods to make them more attractive to the eye, or more palatable – to make margarine spread easily, to stop mayonnaise separating into layers, to colour soft drinks, and so forth. All of these substances are subjected to elaborate testing before they are permitted to be used. *There is no reason to have any doubt about the wholesomeness of foods containing such 'additives'.* Harm is much more likely to arise from eating too restricted a mixture of foods than from the use of these 'additives'.

FOOD POISONING

Food poisoning, as it is generally understood, involves a relatively short period of misery; it usually takes the form of a bout of diarrhoea perhaps accompanied by vomiting, and within a week it is over. Even for adults, however, it can be worse than this. Typhoid, for example, is a kind of food poisoning, and so is undulant fever, which may cause spells of high temperature and prostration continuing for months. But although ordinary food poisoning is disagreeable for adults, it can be downright dangerous for young children. This is what conscientious parents should worry about, rather than about 'chemicals' and 'additives'.

Food poisoning occurs when some articles of food, most commonly meat or a meat dish such as soup, stew, sausages or the like, is contaminated with a harmful germ or 'micro-organism', which has had the opportunity to multiply sufficiently for there to be so many germs that whoever eats the food becomes infected.

Whether or not a food is going to give you food poisoning depends on two things. Firstly, it depends on whether there are any food-poisoning micro-organisms in it or not. Obviously, if there are none it does not matter how decayed it becomes. That is why cheeses covered with mould and crawling with maggots do nobody any harm and are, in fact, nourishing – provided you do not object to the smell. Secondly, even if food-poisoning organisms are present in a piece of meat or a pie, you suffer only *if enough of them are there*. And numbers depend on temperature.

If contaminated food is put in the freezer, the micro-organisms are not killed and can start multiplying whenever the food is taken out and warmed up; but while it is in the freezer the numbers do not increase. The numbers do increase, but only very slowly, when food is stored in a refrigerator. That is why, as everybody knows, food keeps longer in the fridge than it does on the larder shelf.

At very high temperatures, the micro-organisms are killed: so freshly cooked food, provided the cooking has been thorough, will not contain any micro-organisms at all. But when food is neither hot nor cold, i.e. when it is at about blood-heat, it is a source of danger. The longer it stays warm but not hot, the greater is the danger. A few food-poisoning micro-organisms, too few to harm a healthy person, will quickly multiply in, say, a warm sausage roll to become a ravening multitude causing havoc and distress to anyone who eats the food. At such a temperature one germ can become two in 20 minutes; in 40 minutes there are four; in 60 minutes there are eight; in 80 minutes sixteen; in 100 minutes thirty-two, and in 2 hours sixty-four. In 6 hours at this rate – would you believe it? there could be 261,144. So it is very important that left-over foods are cooled quickly so that the dangerous tepid stage is passed as rapidly as possible. Our forebears had the right idea: the cold airy larders of old houses, with their thick slate or marble shelves, were ideal places in which to set the cooling remains of sirloins of beef and legs of pork after the family and the servants had finished their Sunday dinner.

Where food poisoning comes from:

People's hands. There is no use beating about the bush. Most food-poisoning organisms come out of the human anus, and they can be carried into food on the hands of someone who has been to the lavatory and then stepped back into the kitchen without washing. Even if the cook's hands have been washed after attending to the wants of nature, the germs may actually be picked up from a towel or dishcloth on which someone else has wiped contaminated hands. People who have boils or 'poisoned' fingers can also 'poison' any food they handle.

Meat, fish and poultry. Hens and chickens (and sometimes their eggs as well) are often infected with food-poisoning organisms. Pigs, sheep, cattle and fish can also be infected from time to time. This is why it is sensible not to eat raw meat or fish or raw sausages, in which the germs have not been killed by the heat of cooking. Chickens, in particular, present a special risk, because they are often stored and sold frozen. Frozen chickens take a long time to thaw, and the bigger the bird the longer it takes. A housewife in a hurry may not remember to take a bird out of the freezer a whole day – or, for a heavy bird, two days – before she needs to cook it. If any ice remains inside it when it goes into the oven, the inside of the bird will hardly be warm and certainly not hot enough to kill micro-organisms when the outside is already crisp and brown; but the inside is just the part that is likely to be the most heavily contaminated.

Knives, plates and tables. Suppose that the cook cuts up a raw chicken and perhaps takes out its guts with the same knife and then, without washing the knife, leaves it on the kitchen table. When the chicken has been cooked and all the micro-organisms safely killed, the meat can be reinfected if the same unwashed knife is then used to cut it up. The same thing can happen if the cooked chicken is put down on an uncleaned table or plate.

How not to get food poisoning:

The first rule is to keep micro-organisms out of the food. Always wash your hands after going to the lavatory, and dry them on a paper towel or on one of those towels that pull down and then wind themselves up – *never on a dishcloth.* An old-fashioned roller towel that holds germs and then passes them on to the next comer is a dangerous thing to have in a kitchen.

The second rule is to wash any knife or plate or table that might have become contaminated as soon as it has been used and then to wash your hands again.

The third rule is to make sure that any cooked food left over from one meal to be kept for use at another is cooled as quickly as possible and put into a refrigerator or a cool larder – if possible at a temperature of 45°F or lower.

In the next few chapters of this book I shall describe how the simple rules of good nutrition set out in Chapter 1 apply to the specific needs of certain groups – adult men and women, teenagers, children, babies and sick and old people, and to their pets as well – without anyone having to worry or fuss over their meals or to spend money on out-of-the-way items. You may decide to skip some of these chapters for the present: for instance, if you are a woman who cooks and shops for yourself, your husband and your two-year-old twins, you may feel that you can safely postpone reading the chapters about feeding adolescents and elderly people for a year or two. However, find time for them soon if you can; knowledge is never wasted, and the information in them may well prove useful to you in the future.

TWO

Men

'. . . a steady consumption of too much alcohol
may eventually upset the central mechanism
by which appetite is controlled.'

BOTH MEN AND WOMEN are people. To that extent they are the same. It follows, therefore, that in general their needs for food are much the same too. In fact, until they are about nine years old, there is no need to distinguish between them, at least from a nutritionist's point of view. Thereafter, however, there is a difference. On average, women tend to be smaller than men and consequently need less food. On average again, men expend more effort in muscular activity than women do. The 'average' may include a lot of exceptions. There are big women and small men. There are hard-working women and indolent, sedentary men. Men vary, too, from brawny, highly masculine characters to slender, rather feminine individuals, and women vary equally widely. But even with these provisos, men undoubtedly *are* different from women and the differences between them are reflected in a number of different nutritional requirements.

Take Care of Your Heart

Many of the scraps of information which men pick up about what they believe to be 'nutritional science' are either incorrect or irrelevant. I have already pointed out that it is pointless to worry about eating enough vitamins in communities where vitamin-deficiency diseases in grown men and women are rarely or never seen, so that endless arguments about the respective merits of white bread and brown bread or about eggs from battery hens or free-range hens are inapt. But heart disease is another matter. The number of men dying from heart attacks has risen steeply: heart disease now kills about 260 of every 100,000 men between the ages of 45 and 54 in England and Wales and the figure is about 340 for Scotsmen. What is so unfair is that only about 40 *women* of the same age die from heart attacks. Now a man cannot help being a man but he can – by what he eats – do something to save himself from heart attacks. This is no fancy talk about vitamin A in liver or vitamin C in watercress; it is about living or dying.

To a certain extent, dying of a heart attack (or 'coronary') is related to prosperity and good living. It is linked with eating too much and too well, and with living too soft a life. A sensible man can therefore do something to keep himself alive; but there are also some things that lay him open to heart disease about which he can do nothing.

☐ *Being a man.* While this makes him up to ten times as likely as a woman to suffer from a coronary, there is nothing he can do about it.

☐ *Belonging to a susceptible family.* Should a man's father have had heart disease, his uncle have died of it and other members also have had attacks, he is more likely to suffer as well. A man like this can't change his family; but he can reduce his risk by eating sensibly and taking exercise.

☐ *Having high blood pressure (hypertension).* Some people have higher blood pressure than others do, just as some people have thicker necks or longer noses. High blood pressure may, however, develop in later life without people realising what is happening. It may be that no harm may come of it, and if the pressure is dangerously high it can be controlled by drugs. But it is sensible for a man who knows that his blood pressure is above the average to cut down on the amount of salt he eats. This is because hypertension can be made worse by the sufferer eating too much salt (though healthy people have no difficulty in controlling the saltiness of their blood).

☐ *Getting older.* Older men are more likely to have a heart attack than younger men. But no one, in considering the alternative, wants *not* to grow old.

☐ *Suffering from diabetes and gout.* Again, it is hardly a man's fault that he suffers from these ailments. It seems bad luck that they make it rather more likely that he will have a coronary as well.

These five factors, about which a man can do little or nothing, increase his chances of a coronary; but there are five other factors, three of which are concerned with nutrition, which *are* under his control:

☐ *Obesity* increases the chance of a heart attack. If you are affected by any of the first five factors I have listed (or even if you are not) limit the amount you eat to make sure that you do not get fat.

☐ *Cigarette smoking.* Men who smoke cigarettes are more likely to have heart attacks than men who do not. And the more heavily they smoke, the shorter the odds become. You are, of course, free to choose what you want to do and in most places you are free to smoke if you want to. But you should weigh any pleasure you get from smoking against the risks you run by doing so.

☐ *Stress and tension.* Think of a worried man, living on his nerves, tense and on edge and working late night after night, who is determined to succeed and dare not relax lest his competitors, his colleagues or his wife should take advantage of him. Living like this, he is more likely to have a heart attack than he would if, when he got home, he took the dog for a walk, or even stayed at home to read a book or watch television.

☐ *Lack of exercise.* Middle-aged and elderly men who, of all others, are likely to have coronaries, do not need to do press-ups before breakfast or hundred-yard sprints. It is, however, sensible for them to take regular exercise every day – not necessarily strenuous exercise, but if it is sufficient to bring on a moderate sweat, so much the better.

This will help to avoid overweight as well as reducing the risk of a heart attack.

☐ *Fat and eggs.* There is evidence that eating too much fat increases the risk of heart disease. Not all fats are equally dangerous. Unfortunately, however, the fats that people like best and may actually believe to be particularly nourishing are potentially the most hazardous. These are the so-called 'saturated' fats (the word refers to the chemical make-up of the fat). Almost all such fats are of animal origin: they include butter, cream and the fat in milk, lard, dripping and suet, and the fat in beef, mutton and bacon.

I am not saying that all men should give up eating meat, putting butter on their bread and eating chips fried in lard. What I am saying is that if you are an overweight man who takes little exercise, smokes cigarettes and has a relative who has had a coronary (that is, you may have inherited the kind of physique which is susceptible to heart disease) it would be sensible for you to cut down on these animal fats.

People do like fat. Bread and butter is pleasanter than dry bread. Cakes, pastries and pudding contain fat and are desirable foods. Fortunately, however, if you are trying to avoid animal fats, you need not deprive yourself of vegetable fats or of fatty fish like herrings and salmon. Most vegetable oils and fish oils, which chemists call 'polyunsaturated' fats, do not appear to add to the risk of heart disease, so you can with advantage substitute 'soft margarine' for butter, and use oil rather than fat for frying and as a replacement for dripping or lard in cooking.

☐ *Cholesterol and eggs.* There is in all of us, circulating around in our blood, a certain amount of a substance called cholesterol. The precise amount varies from one person to another; but eating too much – and particularly eating too much butter, cooking fat and the fat from meat – tends to raise the cholesterol level in the blood. There is some relationship between cholesterol and coronary heart disease. People who suffer from heart attacks often have rather high levels of cholesterol in their blood.

Of all the common foods, eggs (and within the egg, the yolk) contain the largest proportion of cholesterol. Since eggs can be eaten every day, not only cooked on their own but also as an ingredient of all sorts of cooked dishes, they can also contribute to the level of cholesterol in the blood. It is, therefore, sensible for men who want to take care of their hearts not to eat too many eggs each day.

Oddly enough, brains are even richer in cholesterol than eggs, but since they turn up so seldom on most people's menus the chance of their doing harm is not very great.

Chapter 12 discusses the diet a person ought to eat when he is ill. I have dealt with heart disease here because it is a disease which you can to some degree cause or prevent by what you eat. In this respect, coronary heart disease is similar to obesity, which can also be classified as a 'disease'. Indeed, obesity itself kills; fat people on average don't live as long as thin people do. The manner in which it kills is less dramatic than having a coronary but, regardless of what people may say about fat men being jolly, there is a statistical link between dying early and being overweight. The old saying about people digging their graves with their knives and forks has been proved to be true by the hard actuarial statistics of insurance companies.

Nutrition and Drinking Men

A pint of beer now and then – or even a couple – does not do a man any harm. In fact, if he can afford it and if it puts him in a good humour so that he does not go home and quarrel with his wife, it does him good. And the same holds for a dram of whisky for a Scotsman and a sherry or a gin and tonic for those who like them. Of course, as we have seen, alcohol is a food so that if the drinker's meals supply all the calories he needs, drink taken on top of everything else that he eats can cause him to put on weight.

CIRRHOSIS OF THE LIVER

But when drinking, from being a harmless – nay, a sociable – habit, becomes over-indulgence, nutritional damage can be done. One danger is cirrhosis of the liver; most men have heard of the disease, but often think of it as a joke because you cannot see it as you can some other effects of excessive drinking, such as a red nose or a trembling hand. But cirrhosis of the liver is no joke. It may take up to twelve years to develop, but when it does it can kill. And medical records show that the more they drink the more likely they are to suffer. Here are some figures:

In England and Wales in 1961–5 the average annual consumption of beer, wine and spirits was 5.6 litres a head over the country as a whole; that is roughly the equivalent of five pints of beer every week for every man, woman and child. In the following years, 1964–9, 29 people per million of the population died of cirrhosis of the liver. In 1965–9, people drank a little more, namely 6.0 litres of alcohol, and in 1970–3 rather more people, 33 per million, had cirrhosis of the liver and died.

In France, people drink wine all the time (and this is important – it's not the single 'bender' that kills, but the steady drinking). The average consumption of alcohol in France in 1961–5 was 19.1 litres, and 350 people per million died four years later from liver cirrhosis. And in 1965–9, when the average amount drunk had dropped to 18.1 litres (still three times that of England and Wales) the cirrhosis death-rate four years afterwards for wine-drinking Frenchmen was down to 340 per million (which is more than *ten times* that of mainly beer-drinking Englishmen and Welshmen). It is not that one nation drinks wine and the other beer; the difference lies in the total consumption of alcohol.

ALCOHOLIC MALNUTRITION

Men (and women too) who drink to excess – and particularly those who drink spirits to excess – may give themselves various sorts of malnutrition. One reason is that heavy drinkers develop bad habits. They miss their meals because they are out drinking. Their social life, outside their drinking, crumbles away. Friends no longer ask them out. Their wives eventually lose patience with cooking meals that they do not bother to come home to eat, and stop making the effort.

Moreover, a steady consumption of too much alcohol may eventually upset the central mechanism by which appetite is controlled. Most people's appetite mechanism is set just right so that they always eat almost exactly as much food as they need. Others have an appetite mechanism which only 'switches off' when they have eaten too much, and these are the people who tend to put on weight. In heavy drinkers, on the other hand, the appetite-control mechanism becomes damaged and 'switches off' too early. They lose their appetites and may, if not starve themselves to death, at least eat so little that they run themselves short of one or other of the vitamins they need. A long-term alcoholic may drain himself so completely of vitamin B_1 that he gives himself beriberi, a disease only rarely seen in western countries although it was once common in some tropical areas. Loss of certain other B-vitamins by long-term heavy drinkers can bring on anaemia.

Finally, because alcoholics damage their appetite control and thus eat less and less they may, to complete the vicious circle, become less able to absorb the nourishment from the food they do eat.

Who Needs Meat?

Some industrial workers *believe* that they need meat in order to be able to do a good day's work. Unfortunately for them they have no scientific evidence to support their view. Some years ago, indeed, the Harvard Fatigue Laboratory in the United States organised a rigorous study in which fit young men were given diets providing various amounts of protein. These men were working in jobs like lorry driving, road mending, forestry, carpentry and office work and in kitchens and laundries. At the end of a long trial their fitness was tested by making each man step up on to a 16-in. high platform and down again once every two seconds for five minutes while wearing a rucksack weighted with one-third of his body-weight. At the end of this (if they were able to complete this fairly strenuous test) their pulse rates were measured and other tests of fitness carried out. The scientists could find no connection between their fitness and the protein in their food and whether they ate more or less meat.

In fact, as long as a man eats each day as much as he needs (and he·can tell this better than anyone else) and obtains a proper mixture of foods, extra meat is not going to be of any real help to him. Indeed, since meat always contains a proportion of fat, eating meat may encourage him to consume more fat than he can safely take.

How Many Meals a Day?

The number of meals a man eats each day is very largely a matter of habit. This is shown by the way in which people can become accustomed to a cup of tea at, say, half-past three in the afternoon. If one day the tea-break is delayed until four o'clock or, for some reason, there is no tea at all, complaining voices will soon be heard declaring that everyone is 'dying for a cup of tea'. Similarly, people become used to the accustomed patterns of their other meals.

For instance, it is commonly claimed that 'there is nothing like a good hot breakfast' at the start of the day. Once again, there is very little scientific evidence for this.

Remember, there is another equally widely believed – and equally unscientific – saying that runs: 'Fifty million Frenchmen can't be wrong'. And most of these Frenchmen start the day *without* a good hot breakfast. At best, they eat a roll and drink a cup of coffee. It is also worth remembering that many farm workers do a good deal of work in the early morning *before* their breakfast. When a traditionally minded Briton eats bacon and eggs first thing in the morning he does so not because there is a proven scientific need for bacon and eggs, but because he is used to this kind of breakfast. Not so very long ago in historical terms, we were used to steaks, chops and kidneys appearing on our breakfast tables, but that custom has disappeared and with rising costs bacon and eggs may soon do so too. The main virtue of a hot breakfast is that it encourages a busy person to sit down for a few minutes and eat calmly, rather than in its being hot.

In short, provided a man has enough to eat (but not more), and eats a good mixture of foods, it is of very little importance what the meals are like – whether they are hot or cold, or whether they are eaten early or late. However, there is some evidence, although it is not completely conclusive, that a man's body makes somewhat better use of the nourishment provided by his food if it is split up into a number of meals rather than if it is eaten in the form of one or two big blow-outs.

So what does 'a meal' consist of? One simple definition is that a meal is any occasion when any significant amount of food, drink, or food *and* drink is consumed. Of course, if this definition is used too pedantically, a pint of beer in a pub ranks as 'a meal'. In a nutritional sense this may indeed be true since each pint contributes to the total dietary intake. But even if a meal is defined in a more everyday manner, a great many men do in fact divide their intake into six or more meals a day. For instance, a man may have breakfast (meal 1) before he leaves home. In the mid-morning he will eat a 'snap' or 'piece' (meal 2). Then comes dinner (meal 3), followed by a mid-afternoon tea-break (meal 4), 'tea' (meal 5) when he gets home and perhaps supper (meal 6) before he goes to bed.

The Thin Man's Remedy

There are occasions when a man has become too thin, either after an illness or when he has undergone privation of one sort or another. It may also happen that a man living alone discovers that he has become seriously emaciated. Perhaps he is a student, a bachelor or a widower, and has not been spending enough money on food (either because he has not got it or – and this happens more often than one might suppose – because he is too mean).

The best solution to this problem is to get on friendly terms with a good cook. Firstly, this is likely to help the thin man to eat more food than he ate before. Secondly, he probably begins to eat more fat – in pastries, puddings, cakes and pie-crust, in sauces and cream – and thus increases the energy-value of the food that he does eat. Finally, he is more likely to sit down with a quiet mind and take time over his meals, and that implies that they do him more good than a snack eaten in a hurry off the mantelpiece. And that is true for everyone – man or woman, fat or thin.

To sum up: the science of nutrition is complicated, the list of vitamins necessary for health is long and the tally of essential trace minerals is almost as protracted. Nevertheless, a male citizen of a modern industrial community can select a good diet by following these simple rules:

☐ Get enough to eat, but not so much as to become fat.

☐ Eat a good mixture of foods, combining filling cereal foods and the like with animal foods (and these include fish and eggs), together with fruit and vegetables.

☐ Do not eat too much animal fat.

☐ For the rest, *don't worry*. If the mixture you eat keeps changing, the chances of your nutrition going wrong are slight. Above all, don't be faddy; there is no need.

Women

'... the buxom ladies in Rubens's paintings
would never meet with the approval
of today's slimming magazines.'

WHILE SOME MEN need to take particular care over their diet, women have their special needs as well, and there are certain areas of nutritional science that have a particular interest for them.

The most important differences between the nutritional needs of boys and girls appear at the age of puberty. This is when a girl begins to menstruate, and for the next thirty or forty years the blood she loses each month must be replaced from her diet if she is not gradually to deplete her reserves and thus become anaemic.

The second difference between men and women is that women are in general smaller than men, added to which many of them are also called upon to exert less muscular activity. They are, therefore, if they possess healthy appetites and a taste for good food, more likely to become fat. Since, as another distinction, they are often – although not *always* – vainer than men, they worry more about being obese than men do, even though overweight women have in fact less to worry about than overweight men since they are far less likely to suffer for their obesity by dying of a coronary attack. It is because many women worry so much about being fat that for most of them 'being on a diet' means having to eat less than they like (a hard thing to do) in order to lose weight.

Once a woman is mature, the next stage in her life when she should change her diet to fit her nutritional intake to her special needs is when she switches off her menstrual cycle and becomes pregnant – and I shall have more to say about this in Chapter 8. This stage is linked to the one that naturally follows, when she is breast-feeding her baby. Thereafter, as time goes on, the nutritional needs of a woman progressively become more and more similar to those of a man of the same size.

A woman wishing to understand good nutrition,

whether it is for her own health, for that of her family or for a household of working girls and their friends, can easily be put off by the sheer size of the body of nutritional knowledge. But don't worry. By far the larger part of this knowledge need not concern most people.

What You Need Not Know

Much harm and very little good has been done by expecting ordinary women to understand and, even if they have understood the appropriate textbooks or magazine articles, to remember what kind of a substance each of the vitamins is, how much of it a person needs, and where it comes from. What advantage is a woman to gain from reading in a book on dieting available at a railway bookstall that the daily requirement of vitamin A is 5,000 I.U. or that the requirement of vitamin B_1 (thiamine) is 1–10 milligrams (in fact, 1 milligram a day is enough for almost anyone) and that the food containing it is 'whole grain'? All this is nonsense. If it were the whole truth, then all those millions of people who do *not* eat whole grains would presumably either suffer from beriberi or be dead. In fact, vitamin B_1 turns up in most ordinary foods, so that only those people – mainly the very poor – who eat an exceedingly restricted diet suffer from a shortage of it. Whole grains do contain B_1, but this is of little significance for people who are already getting all the vitamin B_1 they need.

The railway bookstall 'nutrition' book goes on to list the daily requirement of vitamin B_2 (riboflavine) as 50–100 milligrams and that of vitamin B_{12} as 12–50 milligrams – 40 to 60 times too much in the former instance and 10,000 to 50,000 times too much in the latter; that the book in question has been out for ten years and reprinted ten times suggests that in all this time either nobody has understood what the figures meant or, more probably, nobody has paid any attention to them.

The real objection to this sort of approach is, however, that it gives people the idea that the principles of nutrition are complex and incomprehensible or – and this is worse – that good health cannot be attained without eating such unusual commodities as whole grains, yeast, blackstrap molasses or unrefined vegetable oils. *This is not true*. It can.

What You Should Know

A great body of scientific knowledge of vitamins and minerals, fats and proteins and all the other nutrients has come to light during the last hundred years or more. But most people don't think in terms of nutrients but in terms of foods. And to my mind this is sensible, especially for women who so often influence what their immediate families eat. Furthermore, if a woman develops non-sensical ideas about the nutritional magic of honey or the near-theological virtues of bran, not only can she make herself anxious and troubled but the rest of her household.

The first principle of a good diet for the well-fed woman is that, having decided what shape and size she wants to be, she should eat as much food as she needs to achieve such a size and shape *but no more*. If a woman has a tendency to put on weight she knows quite well that she has got to eat less. Everybody knows that fat makes you fat more effectively than other foods because it is the most concentrated of all food ingredients, and that eating chopped cabbage or turnips is eating for amusement rather than nourishment because cabbages and turnips are largely water. This is why articles like sauerkraut and un-sweetened lemon juice are recommended in slimming diets. They provide a way to let yourself eat without really eating very much. And the expensive 'slimming breads' provide less calories than ordinary bread because slice for slice, they weigh less. If, therefore, you want to stay slim it is just as effective – and cheaper – to keep to ordinary bread and to cut smaller slices.

The shape and size a woman wants to be have something to do with nutrition, and so also with health. That is to say, women who decide to be as thin as rakes can damage their health by starving themselves into a state of emaciation. And women who love their food so much that they don't care about their shapes can, if they become really fat, immobilise themselves with varicose veins and run the risk of contracting diabetes.

But women can modify their targets more subtly than this. A farmer keeping a pig can, by the way he feeds it, turn it into a baconer from whose long flat sides rashers of bacon can be sliced, or he can turn the same animal into a porker, more suited to being divided into joints or put through a sausage machine. Similarly, where we ourselves are concerned, it has been said that 'all of us aim to eat the kind of diet best designed to turn us into the sort of people we want to be.' This means that if you want to turn yourself into a champion tennis player you eat from childhood up the kind of diet champion tennis players eat – lots of bacon and eggs, enormous steaks, quarts of milk. On the other hand, if you want to be the shape of a delicate Dresden shepherdess, you eat a moderate delicate diet.

Over the years, the ideals of feminine perfection change. Venus de Milo was a substantial heavyweight with thighs like tree-trunks, and so were the buxom ladies in Rubens's paintings. They would never meet with the approval of today's slimming magazines. There is, however, no evidence to identify any nutritionally 'perfect' set of dimensions. There are standards by which we can make some sort of an assessment of whether or not a person's weight is appropriate to his height and build. But we should not cling fanatically to the idea of a precise perfect weight; rather it is more sensible to accept that there is a broadish range of weights within which you can expect to be healthy. It is within this band that you can choose what shape you want to be, depending firstly on what you like to look like, secondly on the current fashion, and thirdly on what shape your husband (or other observer) fancies.

This then is the first rule for the well-fed woman (as it is for the men in her life): *have enough to eat but not too much*.

The second rule – which must be familiar to you by now: *eat a mixture of foods* (meat, greens and potatoes, cake, bread and butter, cheese now and then, fish) and vary the mixture from day to day, as well as according to the season.

Does 'Quality' Matter?

For most food what is understood by 'quality' is irrelevant to nutrition. Quality in food has nothing to do with food value, just as quality in clothes has nothing to do with whether they keep you warm or not. It's all a matter of style and fashion. Cheap mince is just as nourishing as expensive steak, and fried 'rock salmon' and chips are every bit as good for you as lemon sole and *pommes sautées*. I would go further. A stale egg has just as much goodness as one warm from the hen and certainly there are no more vitamins in a brown egg than a white one.

Iron and Anaemia

Although I am trying to save you from bothering about this vitamin or that, or whether orange juice is better for you than grapefruit (there is almost no difference except in the flavour), it is worthwhile for a woman to take one particular factor seriously. If you follow the basic rules of nutrition, you are not likely to be short of vitamins or anything else. It is possible, however, that you might run low on iron. It is paradoxical that for all those women who worry about vitamins – and even spend good money buying bottles of vitamin tablets at the chemist's without ever having seen anyone suffering from a shortage – few or none bother about iron. Yet anaemia is quite common.

There are several different kinds of anaemia, but the commonest is caused simply by eating too little iron, and may affect as many as one woman in every five. It can be insidious: starting off absolutely fit, you may become just a little below par almost without noticing it, and the condition may gradually worsen long before it would be fair to say you were downright ill.

HOW MUCH IRON DO YOU NEED?

It is hard to say how much iron your diet should contain: no two women need exactly the same amount, mainly because women lose different quantities of blood each month. It is of very little use trying to estimate the *average* menstrual flow and hence the *average* amount of iron a woman needs, since many women lose much more blood than the average figure. So don't worry about counting up milligrams of iron here and there. Just make sure that your diet regularly includes foods that contain the mineral.

In general, there is enough iron naturally present in everyday foods to provide the amount needed to maintain good health. On the other hand, a hard-pressed working woman too rushed to eat proper meals – and among such women can be included the busy working girl, particularly if she fusses about being overweight – may not get enough iron. One of the comparatively few facts of nutrition which *is* worth the ordinary woman's attention is the list of foods that are good sources of iron.

SOURCES OF IRON

Black pudding. Blood sausages are, as you might expect, rich in iron because you need the iron from food as an ingredient of your own blood.

Liver. Liver, and hence liver sausage, is full of all sorts of nutrients (various vitamins, for example) and is also a good source of iron.

Meat of all sorts is a useful provider of iron (oddly enough, corned beef is particularly rich). And meat mixed with other things seems to help the iron in the other ingredients to be better absorbed. You *can* be a well-nourished lady vegetarian but it is easier to be a well-nourished woman by not being a vegetarian.

Black treacle. Nowadays this has become rather an unusual taste. It is, however, a simple inexpensive food. Normally I have not much good to say about 'health foods' but molasses (of which black treacle is merely a particular grade), which is sometimes promoted for its alleged 'health-giving' virtues, is indeed valuable now and then to top up the iron content of a woman's diet. So do not, therefore, think of black treacle only as a food for schoolboys.

Cocoa. Cocoa powder is comparatively rich in iron, so that that bedtime cup of cocoa, although there is only a spoonful of cocoa powder in it, will contribute some iron.

Currants, raisins and sultanas. These are quite rich in iron and although not many people eat particularly large weights of dried fruit, your slice of Christmas cake will add to your total iron intake.

Iron is present in other foods, too, but mostly in very much smaller amounts than in the items in this list. The iron in some foods, however, cannot be taken into the body. For instance, the iron present in spinach (the primary reason why scientists once thought it was so specially nourishing) is largely 'locked up' chemically, so that in fact it does not do much good. Milk contains virtually no iron at all.

Because anaemia due to eating too little iron is so common, the British Government obliges bakers to add a certain amount of iron to white bread. This does not make it as useful a source of iron as, say, meat or liver, but it is reasonable to hope that it helps.

In short, the sensible rule for women who need to replace their monthly loss of blood is to include meat in their weekly menu. Since vitamin C and also one of the B-vitamins, called folic acid, have something to do with the iron being absorbed, it is a good idea to eat greens and potatoes with the meat (the avoidance of potatoes as a 'fattening' food, not to be eaten in any extremity, being recognised as the fashionable nonsense it is).

Nutrition and Your Skin

A woman's diet may sometimes be the cause of her having a bad complexion. Usually, however, diet has little or nothing to do with the matter; though there are several nutritional deficiencies which affect the skin, few people in prosperous countries eat so inadequate a diet that their bad complexions are due to malnutrition. There are dozens of other possible reasons. On the other hand, since individual nutritional needs may differ quite widely from the average, and since there are people, even in countries like Great Britain or the USA, who eat a poor diet, it is worth describing how nutrition *could* affect the skin.

☐ *Roughness of the skin.* Sometimes rough 'goose pimples' develop on the skin of the arms and legs, because the tiny openings through which the little hairs grow become plugged up. These pimples can appear if the diet is lacking in vitamin A. It is not very likely to happen if you eat normally, and the same skin condition can have nothing to do with food but be due to sunburn (or even to too few baths!). But it is worth seeing whether cod-liver oil or halibut-liver oil does any good.

☐ *A whitish 'crust' at the corners of the mouth.* The commonest cause of this is badly fitting false teeth. It *may* be caused, however, by a shortage of one of the B-vitamins (riboflavine) or by anaemia due to too little iron in the diet. If it turns up, therefore, and your teeth are your own, a diet with more iron in it (that is, with black pudding, liver and other meat – or even black treacle) may help. Alternatively, milk and cheese will put up the intake of riboflavine.

☐ *A pale, smooth tongue.* This is hardly a matter of complexion (particularly if you keep your mouth shut) but it may be a sign of bad nutrition. Once again, the most likely nutritional reason is a long-standing lack of iron.

As a general rule, the best recipe for a good skin is good health, although occasionally perfectly fit people have bad complexions for one reason or another. Under conditions of great hardship, when people are starving or suffering from pellagra or some other serious disease of malnutrition, the appearance of their skins shows how ill they are. To most of my readers who live in prosperous western countries, however, the chance of a dietary *deficiency* being the cause of a bad complexion is not very strong. The type of malnutrition they are most likely to see is not a shortage but a surplus of nutrients, by which I mean obesity. Women who eat too much (to put the matter bluntly) besides becoming fat may also suffer from indigestion particularly if, while over-indulging in eating, they also under-indulge in exercise. And you don't need me to tell you that over-fed women who cosset themselves indoors do lose some of the bloom of glowing health that is one of the loveliest characteristics of a good complexion.

What About Your Hair?

One of the indications of the presence of serious malnutrition is a change in the appearance of the hair: glossy black hair, for instance, becomes rusty and 'staring'. It is true that under such conditions a woman is likely to be too much concerned with survival to bother overmuch with her hair. But severe malnutrition of this sort is never likely to afflict you who are reading this book.

An odd piece of recent research may, however, interest women who want not only to be well nourished but also to possess 'healthy' hair. Gelatin, which is made from gristle and the like, is a protein that nutritional scientists are not usually very enthusiastic about. Everyone needs to eat enough protein, and everyone also requires an appropriate mixture of proteins. This mixture is present in most animal products like milk, cheese, eggs and meat, which is why such foods are particularly valuable for children, who need protein to enable them to grow. But although most animal proteins are as good as a mixture of other proteins, gelatin – although of course it is an animal protein – is conspicuously defective as a protein when eaten on its own. There is some evidence, however, that eating gelatin is associated with a thickening of the individual hairs which, it is claimed, makes them easier to comb and curl into aesthetically desirable and fashionable convolutions. This finding, although reported in a reputable journal, has not so far been confirmed. Nevertheless, there would seem to be no harm in an otherwise well-nourished woman eating a daily jelly for a couple of months or so to see whether she thereby thickens her hair.

Losing Your Advantages

Women possess two important physiological advantages over men. One is that they live longer, and thus can expect to outnumber men in any well-conducted old-folk's home. And their second advantage is that they are far less susceptible to coronary heart disease.

In recent years, however, since the ideas of 'women's lib' have come upon the scene, there has been a small but distinct tendency for women who take trouble to behave like men to acquire some of the men's disabilities. That is to say, the 'liberated' women are not outliving men by as many years as their mothers did and, in particular, the number of women suffering from heart attacks – and dying of them – has been rising.

Part of this increased mortality may well be due to nutrition. If women start to indulge in business lunches rich in the fat of juicy steaks, if they begin to share the tension and strain of men who hurry their breakfasts to catch the eight-fifteen to work and snatch a quick ham sandwich at midday, and – most damaging of all – if they smoke too many cigarettes sometimes even *during* meals (as they increasingly do) it is not surprising if, even though fewer women may still die of heart disease than men, the gap will begin to close.

Virtues of Marmalade Sponge

Not long ago, a radio commentator remarked upon a survey which showed that marmalade sponge, apple crumble, and prunes and rice were still – as they have been for ages – among the most popular puddings in industrial canteens. He made supercilious noises in his surprise that working men and women should actually like to eat what he described as 'stodge'. But what the incident really showed was the commentator's ignorance of the basic principles of the science of nutrition.

Because of the comparative wealth of modern industrial communities, it has come to be regarded as axiomatic that good nutrition must always imply eating less. This may not be so. Prosperous women without family responsibilities often enjoy high salaries and jobs that involve sitting down working peacefully at a desk all day; if so, it is easy for them to eat more than they need and consequently put on weight. For them the problem *is* to eat less, which they can most readily do by filling themselves up with foods like grapefruit, lettuce and tomato which are mostly water. On the other hand, some women need to expend a considerable amount of physical energy every day. If they are silly, they may believe that salads and thin slices of 'slimming' rusks are the only way to obtain a satisfactory diet. They may even come to believe the magazines which imply that by making themselves bony, drawn and emaciated they can become beautiful and fashionable.

Obesity and the associated 'slimming' craze are impor-

tant, I suppose, to people who are suffering – yes, suffering
-- from affluence and physical indolence. There are,
however, very many women who work hard, and by work I
mean muscular labour, in factories and shops, in transport
and catering, in hospitals and farming; many women work
hard, for long hours, at home, and many more work hard
both at home *and* in outside industrial employment. To
keep going, these women must have *enough to eat*. And Pam
Ayres's heartfelt lines speak for all those who *need* the
energy-value in marmalade sponge and suet duff rather
than a little pot of fat-free quince-flavoured yogurt:

> *Oh bring back the roly-poly pudding,*
> *Bread and butter pudding . . . Spotted Dick!*
> *Great big jugs full up of yellow custard,*
> *That's the sort of pudding I would pick.*

Of all the rules of nutrition, the basic and most
important one is to fill up the tank with enough fuel to keep
the engine going, or, in scientific terms, to consume
enough calories to enable the day's work to be done
without having to call on the body's reserves. It is nonsense
to believe that only salads, fruit desserts and pure orange
juice are good for you, while the excellent tasty puddings of
old times are 'rubbish' or 'stodge'. They're not. It all
depends on *what you need*. There are probably as many
hard-working women who ought to eat more than they do
as there are fat ladies who are trying to get thin, and who
find that it's tough having to leave the table hungry while it
is still loaded with good things to eat. But it is worse having
to leave the table hungry because there is not anything
more to eat, or because one is too tired and busy to cook it.

This brings me back again to the importance of
bread. If a woman has plenty of money she will probably
choose to buy a joint of meat every week and her diet will be
made up from foods like bacon and eggs, toast, marmalade
and orange juice for breakfast, with a cooked lunch,

perhaps, of meat, vegetables and sweet, and maybe fried fish or even another full meal in the evening. But as money becomes scarce, the bacon, the meat and the fish will begin to take up more of the weekly budget than can be spared. The first economy will probably be the replacement of the cooked midday meal by sandwiches: that is to say, the body's basic need for fuel will be met by bread. Then the full cooked evening dinner will be replaced by a high tea. Nutritionally, this can be every bit as good as a more elaborate menu, provided the mixture of items is kept diverse. But again, more expensive animal foods are replaced by bread.

But if bread became expensive or if for some reason – perhaps a strike or, worse still, a war – bread and flour became scarce, then indeed people's nutrition might be under threat. In the east, rice takes the place of bread but in the west it is usually more expensive, calorie for calorie, than bread and we are not accustomed to it. At one time, Scottish crofters used to keep themselves going on oatmeal, and the impoverished Irish peasants on half a dozen pounds of potatoes a day. But today neither the Scots nor the Irish would thank their governments if oats and potatoes were the only available foods. We look for better things nowadays. But when times are hard and money is short we shall do quite well if we base our diet on bread *provided* there is some meat to put into the sandwiches and lettuce and tomato as well, and butter to spread on the bread – and an educated public-health system to see that vitamins are added to the margarine if butter (another animal food) becomes dear as well. Like this, bread becomes the foundation of a well-balanced diet in a way that no other food can match.

Slimming diets can be interesting topics of conversation and it may seem modern and sophisticated to talk about B-vitamins in wheatgerm and amino-acids in honey (even without properly understanding what these substances do or whether the amounts present are worth bothering about). The first principle of nutritional science, however, is getting enough to eat, and even today, when things become tough, bread can still be a very important basic food, and one that lies at the heart of the science of nutrition.

Some time ago, a strike of bakery deliverymen was causing a bread shortage. 'There is no need to worry,' a so-called 'expert' purred soothingly from the broadcasting studio, 'failing bread, people can obtain their nutritional energy equally well from beans, potatoes or peanuts.' It was a comment that illustrated how basic and widespread is the ignorance of nutrition, and how even relatively well-informed people can be unaware of the fundamental importance of an everyday food like bread.

And Children

'Marble chips contain a lot of calcium
yet it might not be a particularly good idea
to mix them with the cornflakes.'

THERE ARE STILL PARENTS who regard their children as greedy little pigs, always eating yet always complaining of hunger. But can you deny that when *you* were a child you were capable of raiding the store-cupboard when no one was around to stop you? In fact, the hearty appetites of healthy children show their special nutritional requirements.

There are three reasons why children need more to eat in proportion to their size than grown-up people.

The first reason is that children need food to enable them to grow. In terms of energy-value, each ounce of flesh they put on needs about 130 calories-worth of food to build it – the equivalent of about one slice of bread and butter – on top of the food that is used up as fuel.

The second reason is that a child's body generally operates at a faster rate than an adult's. He therefore needs proportionately more energy-value in his food than adults do. The younger the child, the greater is his relative need for energy to keep his body going; during his first year of life a child burns up more than twice as much food energy for each pound of his body weight as his father does.

Finally, normally healthy schoolchildren expend far more energy in proportion to their size than adults do. Children race to and from and jump and punch each other, where adults walk sedately. Children rush up and downstairs, they turn somersaults and handstands, they scuffle and romp around. They play football and hockey, they ride bicycles and tumble about on skateboards. All this calls for fuel, and the fuel can only come from food.

The first principle guiding those responsible for feeding children must be to ensure that they have *enough to eat*. Because children are smaller than adults and possess smaller stomachs their food must provide a reasonably *concentrated* source of energy. How is this to be done?

☐ Fat is the most concentrated of all the foods and children enjoy it as an ingredient of cake, as the fat or oil in which chipped potatoes or fish are fried, as butter or margarine on their bread and, in my day at least, as the dripping that constituted the particularly delicious quality of bread and dripping. They do not always like fat *as fat*. I suspect that this is why they so often like sugar instead.

☐ Sugar, besides being sweet, is also a very concentrated source of energy-value. Children like sweet things both because of their sweetness *and* because of their energy-value. It is fashionable to decry sugar, and it is quite true that *too much* sugar would unbalance any diet. But when a schoolboy piles strawberry jam (which is mostly sugar) on to his roly-poly and when his sister ladles extra golden syrup on top of two slices of treacle tart, they are following the first principle of child nutrition and making sure that they get enough to eat in the concentrated form they need, so that as soon as they rise from the table they can dash down the road to play.

☐ Boys and girls like steamed puddings and Spotted Dick for the excellent reasons that they are made of such concentrated ingredients as flour and fat.

☐ Foods that are mostly water fill up children's stomachs without providing much energy-value. So don't give children big bowls of thin soup, for instance; if they are to have soup at all, let it be the kind that is crammed with meat and beans so as to form a whole meal in itself.

Eating Between Meals

Generations of parents and schoolrooms-full of teachers have scolded children for eating between meals. Although children can survive a world of scolding without coming to much harm, it is my opinion that in general the children have been right to eat between meals and their parents in the wrong. Since active growing children require plenty of food and since their stomachs are comparatively small, they need to obey the urge to top up their fuel supply with what amounts to supplementary meals.

Of course children, like anybody else but more than most, need to obtain more from their food than energy. This is why – as sensible mothers know perfectly well – they would soon fall ill if they tried to live on *nothing but toffee*, which is made from fat and sugar, two highly concentrated sources of energy-value, and why it is obviously silly to allow them to suck one toffee after another the whole afternoon through so that they are unable to eat any tea. Besides, this kind of indulgence is bad for their characters.

Several scientists have tried to find out what children *do* eat between meals if left to themselves, and these studies have shown that they go for apples and pieces of cake (containing such nourishing ingredients as eggs, butter and flour), raisins, cheese and potato crisps. And the compositions of some of these mixtures were found to provide quite a good balanced mixture of proteins, vitamins and minerals, not to mention the energy-value which attracted the hungry youngsters to eat in the first place.

Obviously parents need to be sensible. The between-meal snacks ought not to comprise too many sweets and sugary soft drinks. All the same, a good diet depends on a sensible mixture being chosen within a period of, say, a week. The ingredients of a single snack or meal are not important of themselves, but only so far as they contribute to the mixture as a whole.

Fat Children

The 'scientific' books on nutrition and the solemn magazine articles give tables showing the number of calories required by an 'average' child of five to seven years old, or of seven to nine years old. Then they give figures specifying the needs of 'average' boys of nine to twelve, twelve to fifteen, and fifteen to eighteen, and another set of figures for girls. These figures are all very well for people responsible for laying in food stocks for a city-full of children but they are not much help to anyone anxious to get things right for a particular boy or girl. After all, there is no such thing as an 'average' child. If there were, we should never be able to pick out our own particular little horrors in a crowd.

If a healthy adult puts on weight, then he is clearly consuming too many calories; if he is losing weight he is consuming too few; and if his weight remains stationary then he is having just about the right amount of food. Things are not quite so easy with children because their food must not only provide them with the energy to make their systems go and keep them going; it has also to enable them to grow, though not so much that they become really overweight.

With so much fuss being made about fat people and so much attention being paid to so-called 'slimming' foods, 'health' farms (as if the dairy and pig varieties were unhealthy), clubs for 'WeightWatchers' and the like, it is not surprising that some of all this should have spilled over on to the children. There are indolent inactive children who stuff themselves with food and become fat. And there is some evidence that really obese children tend to grow up into obese men and women. But there are not too many of these. After all, Billy Bunter is about as uncommon in real life as he was in the stories in which he appeared. While, therefore, it is sensible not to force a schoolchild to eat so much cream and butter, so many fried eggs and chips, and so much sweet cake covered in chocolate icing as to become grossly fat, it is also sensible not to worry unduly at having a plump child. It is particularly unwise for a mother, just because she may be 'slimming' herself, to fancy that the children would necessarily benefit from a 'slimming' diet as well.

☐ During their growing period both boys and girls often pass through a chubby phase. This does not necessarily mean that they will grow up into fat men and women. In a year or two the phase may pass, and they will most likely 'grow out of it'.

☐ There is nothing at all wrong with active schoolboys and schoolgirls who are big eaters and sometimes seem to want to eat all the time, provided that they eat, overall, a varied mixture of foods; they *need* the food.

☐ While it is bad for children to be fat, it is not good nutrition to institute a 'slimming' diet for them too hastily. 'Slimming' – for them as for anyone else – means cutting back the amount of food they eat.

☐ Rather than cutting back their food too drastically, it is good sense and good nutrition as well to make sure that children are active. There is no need to encourage most healthy youngsters to take exercise: they hop and skip about readily enough, running when an adult would walk and generally behaving like the children they are. Some schoolchildren, however, *are* lazy, and if such children are ferried to and from school in the family car, excused from school sports and allowed to sit in an armchair watching television all evening, they may become really fat.

Remember too that though some older people believe that their schooldays were the happiest time of their lives, when you are young schooldays can be exceedingly unhappy; and to the fresh sensitive mind of youth unhappiness can be more painful than at any time later on. And one reaction to such melancholy can be to sit about instead of playing or working, *and to eat*. Should this be seen the caring parents will try to ease the sorrow if they can, and will help to maintain nutrition and avoid obesity by encouraging the child to take exercise.

What Children Should Eat

The main way in which schoolchildren's needs differ from those of adults is that the children are growing, so that their food must provide the substance from which flesh and bone can be made, in addition to their other needs. And this brings us to *protein*.

In communities like ours, almost all the talk and attention devoted to protein is irrelevant, unnecessary and for the most part misleading as far as adults are concerned. If an ordinary citizen gets enough to eat he can hardly fail to consume not merely as much protein as he needs, but more like twice as much. There is no harm in this. The spare protein is used up as fuel and does no more and no less good than an equivalent amount of fat, sugar or starch. Although children, like adults, can hardly fail to consume enough protein if they get enough to eat (unless they try to live on nothing but soft drinks and bullseyes), for them it is not solely a matter of eating *enough* protein: it is also important to get *enough of the right kind of protein*.

Now no two proteins are *exactly* alike: cheese proteins, beef proteins, pea proteins and so forth are all different. But when any protein is digested in a person's stomach and intestines it is taken apart into twenty or so different chemical 'bits'. These 'bits' soak through the sides of the guts into the bloodstream. A growing schoolchild's body has to make a selection from all the 'bits' that have been derived from the various proteins in the child's meals – proteins in bread, milk, meat, potato chips, baked beans, fish fingers, boiled eggs and all the rest; then it puts the 'bits' together to make boy proteins or girl proteins as the case may be. In fact, so artfully is the reconstruction done that the new protein becomes a special protein peculiar to that one boy or girl, *and to no other*.

Now although there is plenty of protein in a simple cheap diet of bread and butter, cabbage soup and plum duff (the sort of diet that Oliver Twist did not get enough of), the body of a growing schoolchild has quite a problem to put together the 'bits' of protein from this diet into human-body protein. And the children who sat down to table with Oliver could not therefore grow as fast, and consequently as much, as they might have done.

Early in this century, the children in hard-up families often lived mainly on bread and jam or bread and dripping, and even if the family could afford a joint of meat once a week, the children might not be given much of it, if any. Scientific trials showed that the growth and health of schoolchildren improved significantly if they were regularly given milk. This was, in fact, the basis of the milk-in-schools schemes which have been in operation in one form or another ever since.

Nowadays we know that if bread is the main source of protein for a growing boy or girl, although it can provide *enough* protein, the protein supplies *cannot easily or quickly* be turned into boy- or girl-protein. If, however, the 'bits' of protein come from a mixture of bread protein and milk protein, the combination of the two *can* readily be fitted together to make child-muscle protein. And this was how, in those feeding trials of fifty years ago, the children given milk grew taller and heavier than those left on the diet based mainly on bread.

Things are different today. It is generally agreed that if a child of five to eleven years old eats the foods that most children eat in modern industrial communities, and is given half a pint of milk a day from all sources – that is, from tea, cornflakes, yogurt, pudding or just as milk to drink – then additional milk is unlikely to do him any more good. On the other hand, provided a child's diet is carefully put together to provide a mixture of bread, beans, potatoes and greens (some meat, fish or cheese as well, of course, helps the mixture) and provided there is enough of it, he can grow and thrive perfectly well without any milk at all.

Milk is undoubtedly a useful food. For infants, it is *very* useful, and it is also handy in helping bones to grow. Obviously, the skeletons of growing boys and girls must keep up with the rest of them. But while milk is useful in its place, it is not a magical food. When money is scarce there is, therefore, no need to buy it *at all cost*.

School meals

Good school meals are valuable, firstly, because they 'top up' the pupils' need for energy. While most children show a reluctance to go to bed at night and often stay up longer than their parents think is good, at least an equal number show a corresponding unwillingness to get up in the morning. The result is that there is often a breathless rush to get dressed, collect any necessary sports gear and books and set out for school. And the results of sleeping late and hurrying out of the house at the double like this is that many children reach school in the morning without having had very much to eat. And for children like these, school dinners bridge the long hours before they return home for their evening meals.

While some children leave home without having any breakfast at all, others snatch a piece of bread or toast, smear it with butter, slap on a spoonful of marmalade – and that's that. In some families father leaves the house early before the children are dressed, *and* mother goes off to work too, merely shouting 'Hurry up!' as she slams the front door. It takes a very sensible child (as well as a kitchen full of food) to prepare itself a good mixed breakfast under these circumstances.

It is only a minority of children who settle down to a meal providing a good and nutritious mixture – say, an apple, an orange or some orange juice, followed by an egg, or egg and bacon (at the price bacon can be!) or egg, bacon, sausage and tomato (an almost perfect mixture). And for many schoolchildren, therefore, school meals usefully broaden the daily mixture of foods, so that they eat potatoes and vegetables, meat and cheese, as well as enough to satisfy their hearty appetites.

What Children Actually Eat

Schoolchildren are not always wise and prudent in choosing what they want to eat. Too many, for example, have acquired an addiction to sweets and to sweetened soft drinks through misguided indulgence by parents in their early years. But when children cut themselves big slices of home-made cake they show a natural instinct for fulfilling their need for an excellent mixture of wheat protein (from the flour) and egg protein from the eggs that are part of any good cake recipe.

Beans on toast, popular with children though often sneered at by supercilious adults, also contribute an admirable combination of wheat protein from the toast and bean protein from the beans.

When I was a boy, ice-cream was also frowned on though the mixture of milk powder, fat, sugar (and bubbles) contributes quite a number of useful nutrients including protein. The objection in my day was probably based on the idea that if the children liked it, it must be bad!

The British sausage, joke though it has become, represents an almost ideal way of providing different kinds of protein to children who not only use protein in growing but also usually like sausages. It is, in fact, a mixture of chopped-up meat and bread (the sausage manufacturers like to call the stuff they mix with their meat 'rusk', but it is actually bread – and none the worse for that). Sausage and mash is even better, providing a mixture of cereal protein from the 'rusk', potato protein from the mashed potato, and meat protein from the meat. As with the other protein mixtures – cake, beans on toast, ice-cream – the nutritional value of the mixture of protein is greater than that of ingredients taken separately.

The second point to remember about protein is that milk and cheese, eggs and fish, liver and bacon, beef, mutton, veal and pork, turkey and chicken – all these have a good deal of protein in them. If, therefore, your particular schoolboys and schoolgirls *like* these foods – and most of them do – and if you can afford to provide them, you can instantly cease to worry about protein. Big meat-eaters (or eaters of fish, eggs, poultry or rabbits – let's not leave them out) will consume much more protein than they need, whether they are youngsters or adults.

GROWING BONES

If the house catches fire and is burnt to ashes and you with it, the firemen who carefully examine what is left of you will find that none of the flesh remains. In the heat of the fire all the muscles and sinews, the lights and liver will have gone up in smoke. What is left, however, is the skeleton — skull, bones and teeth – as white as chalk. And the reason why it will be as white as chalk is that – roughly speaking, and provided the fire has been hot enough – it will *be* chalk. The main chemical component of chalk is calcium. And since 'we are what we eat', the calcium in our skeletons comes from our food.

Now an ordinary good mixed diet contains quite enough calcium in it to keep the bones of an adult going and is almost always enough to allow the bones of a growing schoolboy or schoolgirl to grow. Milk is particularly rich in calcium and, as you might guess, cheese is too. But even though in a reasonably prosperous industrial community – and particularly in one like Great Britain, where the public-health authorities insist that chalk be added to white bread flour – boys and girls will probably obtain all the calcium they need from their everyday food, it is a useful insurance to give schoolchildren cheese and perhaps from time to time more than the daily half-pint of milk I spoke of earlier.

There is another point, however, to be borne in mind. Not only must calcium be present in the children's food: they must also be able to absorb it. Marble chips contain a lot of calcium yet it might not be a particularly good idea to mix them with the cornflakes. Similarly oyster shell, which is also full of calcium, is quite commonly given to hens before they start to lay their eggs, to meet the birds' need for extra calcium to make eggshell out of; but large flakes of oyster shell would obviously be an unsatisfactory source of calcium for boys and girls.

It is in this matter of absorbing calcium that vitamin D is so useful to the young, because it pulls the calcium in food through from the digestive system into the bloodstream and thence to those places where it is needed, including the ends of the growing bones. Most children have no difficulty with their vitamin D supply. If those in charge of them know their business, they will be given cod-liver oil, halibut-liver oil or some other concentrated source of vitamin D when they are small. And when they go to school the butter and margarine, the milk and the herrings and kippers they eat will provide them with the necessary trickle of the vitamin to top up what remains from their boyhood, some of which will have been tucked away in their livers for a rainy day. In addition, whenever they run about in the sunshine more vitamin D will be made in their skin.

VITAMINS

People trying to teach nutrition usually make too much fuss about vitamins, about what you must and must not eat, and about what you ought and ought not to do with a cabbage when you boil it. By and large, however, all that needs saying is *vary the mixture and your diet will be all right*. But where children are concerned, it is worth remembering that they can run themselves short of one vitamin or another more quickly than grown-ups do. Besides, children need relatively greater amounts of vitamins than their elders require. With this in mind, it is good practice to make sure that schoolchildren eat potatoes and greens that have not been overcooked or kept hot, or apples, oranges or other fresh fruit in season, and drink orange juice that guarantees on its label that it has vitamin C in it (and this may easily leave out some of the orangeades and squashes and pops the kids drink), and that they have these foods, if not each day, then certainly two or three times a week.

No vitamin pills

Provided, then, that schoolchildren eat a sensible mixture of foods at mealtimes, with perhaps the odd ice cream, apple or chocolate bar (though this last is probably a waste of money and there should not be too many of them), and provided that during a week's eating they eat reasonable helpings of vegetables or fruit (or both), then there are two good reasons for *not* spending money buying vitamin pills for them.

The first reason is that the less money there is to spend on food, the easier it is to give the wrong food or – if the worst comes to the worst – give too little food to a growing boy or girl. The wrong diet usually comes from its being too narrow a mixture. Meat, vegetables and fruit may seem dear, and it may seem easier to satisfy those enormous appetites with bread and jam. Eggs, fish, liver and bacon – all things that usefully diversify the mixture – may be dropped because they are felt to be too expensive. Since money is a very important factor in the provision of a good diet, it is stupid to waste it on unnecessary trimmings such as vitamin pills.

But there is another reason. Too much of some of the vitamins – vitamin A is one example – can be poisonous.

There have been enthusiastic mothers who have spent good money buying halibut-liver oil, of which two or three *drops* provides all or more of the vitamin A anyone could possibly need, and who have given their children two or three *spoonfuls*. In a short time the children lose their appetites, become cross and irritable, their skin becomes dry and itchy, and swellings come up over the bones of their legs and arms.

The moral is clear. It is much better to nourish schoolchildren by feeding them good food than by giving them pills.

Eating When Ill

It is often said that healthy schoolchildren 'eat anything' – and so they should. A boy of five, when in the mood, will eat a hunk of cheese right off that would satisfy a working man. And if schoolboys and schoolgirls chop and change, so much the better.

But children are not always healthy. Mothers know very well that a boy or girl starting school for the first time is sure to bring 'something' home. In these days of vaccination and inoculation it is not measles, mumps, chickenpox, German measles, whooping cough and scarlet fever as often as it used to be in my young days; but there are plenty of alternatives. Apart from the varieties of influenza that crop up each year, there is a whole series of vague fevers that are transmitted from one child to another. Fortunately, many of the infections children pick up soon pass, provided they have proper treatment. Part of such treatment is a good diet. And feeding a sick child follows the same principles as feeding a healthy one, with certain modifications.

A child with a high temperature feels ill and wants to lie as still as his discomfort will allow until the fever passes off. Because he does not want to exert himself even in eating, his food should be provided in a form that requires very little trouble to eat. This means that it should mostly be liquid.

Yet *because* the child is ill with fever, which does actually cause the body to 'waste away', it is particularly important for the food that is eaten to be *more* nourishing than what a normal child would need to eat, and this is especially true if the fever lasts for more than a day or two.

The first thing to do is to provide plenty to drink, partly to replace the moisture the hot restless child loses as sweat. Fruit juice sweetened with sugar will provide both the vitamin C and also some of the energy-value which normally would come from all the varied foods fit children with good appetites eat. Orange or lemon juice with water and sugar added are every bit as good as those much more expensive drinks that are advertised on television.

A sensible breakfast for a child in bed with a temperature is what our grandparents called gruel. This could be strained porridge made liquid by adding milk and sugar, plus milk as a drink with some sugar in it to add to its energy-value.

Since sick children have poor appetites, it is a good idea to supply 'elevenses' as well, comprising a hot milky drink, or perhaps an egg beaten up in milk or in orange juice.

Dinner at midday could usefully be strained soup (the straining makes it easier to take) or scrambled egg, custard or even cheese omelette, with perhaps more milk as junket.

For supper, minced chicken or fish with white sauce followed by, say, jelly with a sponge finger and milk to drink would serve to keep the nourishment going without calling for much effort by the sick child. And another milky drink, perhaps flavoured with chocolate, last thing at night would help to get the child with little appetite to consume more than he otherwise could manage.

A feverish child often sweats plentifully, and is losing salt from his system in his sweat, so that whoever prepares his food must not forget to put salt into the scrambled egg, the soup and even the gruel.

GETTING BETTER

While most children catch diseases easily and go down abruptly with sudden fevers, the causes of which are sometimes quite obscure, they often recover equally quickly. Today, doctors have at their disposal a great many potent healing drugs, of which the antibiotics are perhaps the most remarkable (when my own father died of tuberculosis in his fifties, children and young people were dying of it too; but for many years now most of the old TB hospitals have been closed and the buildings demolished or put to other uses). Many children's diseases are now short-lived. And the first sign that a child is getting better is that he begins to be hungry again.

The most sensible response to the child's restored appetite is to return to the healthy mixed diet that he normally eats, carefully and gradually. Some children throw off their ailments quickly and are ravenously hungry again almost at once. But in others the appetite returns only slowly. In a case like this, a mother's special knowledge of her particular child and his favourite dishes can often suggest appropriate tricks to tempt him into eating again.

AFTER THE ACCIDENT

Schoolchildren break their bones as a result of falling out of trees or of reckless bicycle riding, rough games or general silliness. As a result they may have to stay in bed for weeks or months, rather than days. The trouble is that lying in bed for any extended period of time causes some of the calcium from the bones to dissolve away and become lost in the urine – a curious fact first discovered by research scientists and later confirmed by astronauts who do most of their travelling lying down or, at best, floating about on a sort of air-cushion. It is, therefore, good nutrition to give *plenty of foods which are rich in calcium* to a child who must be kept in bed for a long time: milk and cheese are easy to give, and if canned salmon is on the menu the child can be encouraged to eat the backbone. It is also sensible to give such children *plenty to drink* to prevent the calcium they do lose from silting up their kidneys.

When to Scold and Love

In this brassy society of ours, it happens all too often that when the kids get up from the television set and head for the front door and their parents ask 'Where are you going?' the answer they receive is 'Out'. Worst of all, some parents are prepared to accept this as a sufficient answer.

But children's health and happiness are dependent partly on a sensible and properly integrated intake of calories, protein, vitamins and minerals they need, and partly also on having the support of living in a sensible and properly integrated community. And the most important part of the community is the family.

A child by the time he goes to school is already a complex personality. To be healthy, the child needs to eat his food. While it is good for him to eat a due proportion of, say, greens there is no need to scold if now and then he does not. But if your child consistently refuses greens and fruit – or meat and cheese, maybe – it is a good idea to find out why. And if the reason appears to be pure cussedness, then there are two good reasons why you should lay down the law, exercise due discipline and, if necessary, scold until the little perisher does as he's told. They are:

☐ A little parental firmness early on may instil good nutritional habits and avoid silly fads appearing.

☐ Scolding, provided it is done with love, will show the child that he matters – that, in fact, you *do* care for him. Such a feeling of being cared for contributes materially to his happiness (and hence to his health) and it can also prevent food fads developing. Children who refuse to eat what is good for them may do so because they are unhappy or uncertain of themselves. They are, even when quite young, conservative in their outlook. If, therefore, when feeling lonely or uncared-for, they decide (without consciously knowing why) that they don't like cheese – or orange juice, or milk – they may start a habit which, even when they have acquired more insight, will be difficult to break.

Here then is some good nutritional advice:

Sometimes schoolchildren need persuading and tempting; sometimes it *is* worth telling them that rice pudding with milk, or orange juice, or boiled eggs or beef is good for them. (It is not often necessary to have to wheedle them into knowing that ice cream is good for them too.) In fact, love is a useful ingredient of a nutritionally satisfactory diet.

On other occasions schoolchildren need to know who is the boss. Discipline and judicious reproof (call it scolding if you like) are out of fashion nowadays, but they too can be valuable components of good nutrition. Almost all children have a hunger for properly administered direction. Provided they know that the one who scolds both really loves them and also knows what he or she is talking about, in their hearts they understand the value of the scolding and at the same time learn to eat properly.

There is no need to scold (or try to persuade) to such a degree as to nag. Children's likes and dislikes come and go. For example, fishbones hurt children's mouths more than they do those of their elders, so that as they grow up they may well forget their earlier dislike of herrings. It may be annoying to have the kids refuse the fish (or the Brussels sprouts) you have been to a lot of trouble to buy, prepare and cook, but they are not going to go down with a nutritional deficiency disease if they don't eat them. Remember, the ideal mixture is not required *every day*; make up the mixture by serving meat (or garden peas) to replace the fish (or the sprouts) later in the week.

THREE

Small Fry

'Young children do develop these likes and dislikes
and may go through phases when all they seem to want to eat
is banana . . .'

ALTHOUGH after about his first birthday a child can perfectly well share most of the things that the rest of the family eats, at that age he possesses not only a smaller body than his parents', but a body of quite different proportions. The most striking difference is that the head of a young child represents a far larger proportion of its total height than does that of an adult. And *because* a toddler's head constitutes so large a proportion of its frame, its stomach is by that very fact far smaller in proportion than an adult's. When young children are given a diet which, though bulky, does not provide the nourishment they need, one of the first things that happens is that they develop sadly grotesque pot-bellies from trying to stuff enough of the poor-quality food into a stomach not big enough to hold it.

See How They Grow

Everybody knows that healthy little children grow, and that a child's diet ought to be so constituted that it enables him to grow more or less steadily until he turns into a full-sized adult. Just the same, all children (like all grown people) are different. Although it is only natural for you to compare your little boy with the one next door, there is no need to worry if, when you put him back to back with the other kid, he turns out to be smaller (unless there is something obviously wrong and little Willy has stopped growing altogether for perhaps a whole year). Equally, your feeding schedule need not necessarily be all that wonderful, just because your child is bigger than your neighbour's.

Moreover, children do grow remarkably quickly, and they grow fastest when they are babies and toddlers: a child's weight will increase by about a quarter between his first and second birthdays, but thereafter the rate drops off rapidly. It is during this stage, therefore, that you have to take special care to make sure that their food must be sufficiently concentrated and, because of their very small stomachs, that it comes to them as a series of small, nourishing meals, avoiding too much watery food like thin soup and jelly. And even then, they can usefully have snacks between their meals, as long as the snacks are themselves good nourishing food like cheese or cake. Above all, it is important to make sure that small children get enough protein, and the easiest way to provide them with plenty of protein is to give them milk, particularly since this supplies calcium to their growing bones as well.

Giving Them Milk

Milk, which is designed by nature to make little cattle (that is calves) grow, is also particularly useful and convenient in making little children grow. It *is* possible for children to do without it or to make good progress with comparatively little but in most well-organised communities it is readily available, and it is sensible to give it to them. Children between the ages of one and five years can use a pint or so every day. There is no harm in giving them more provided that they still have room for the other more concentrated foods they need, such as eggs and meat, bread and butter, as well as fruit and vegetables.

If a child likes cheese, cheese is a good way of providing him with protein and calcium without filling up his little stomach with the water that milk contains, and yogurt, which has become popular, also provides most of the nourishment of milk.

Don't take risks

In properly organised towns nowadays, the milk sold by

the milkman is always pasteurised. This is as it should be. Sometimes, perhaps during an idyllic country holiday, the idea comes to mind that milk straight from the cow is a good thing to give young children. It is not. Raw milk is no more nourishing than properly pasteurised milk and is always potentially dangerous. One reason is that cows can suffer from certain diseases that can be transmitted to children. The most serious of these is tuberculosis. But even milk from a herd that has been turberculin-tested (so-called 'TT') may be able to infect people with *brucellosis*. This can give a child a septic throat or even *undulant fever*, which is much more difficult to throw off. Besides this, some cows carry the micro-organisms responsible for food poisoning, and while this may be a nuisance to adults, it can be dangerous to small children. Pasteurised milk is safe milk; the bacteria carrying all these diseases are killed by the pasteurisation process.

Raw milk is dangerous too because, just as it is a nourishing food for young people, it is equally attractive to young bacteria and it makes *them* grow and multiply too. At every stage in its passage from the cow's udder (which, it must be admitted, is situated uncomfortably near the place where the cow's droppings come from) to the pail or container, to the churn or tank it is stored in, and so on to the bottle or jug in which it reaches the breakfast table, milk can pick up dirt and infection from the cow, from infected milk with which it may be mixed, from the utensils, or from the coughing dairyman who handles it. Pasteurisation kills off any harmful bacteria that may have reached the milk by these routes.

In short, no responsible parents should ever risk infecting their children, particularly when safe, pas-teurised milk is readily available.

FEEDING WITHOUT MILK

If milk is not available it is possible – but much more

difficult – to feed young children properly. Of course, if cheese and yogurt are obtainable there is no problem. They are virtually the equivalent of milk. Powdered dried milk is also an excellent food for children. The reason why it is usually labelled NOT TO BE USED FOR BABIES is because it is generally made from skimmed milk, not because it is unwholesome in itself. Milk with the cream taken off it has less energy-value than whole milk. Since babies have to obtain virtually the whole of their diet from milk, they may not be able to get enough to eat if they are only given skimmed milk. Besides, skimmed milk does not supply vitamin A or, what is more important, vitamin D, without which babies may develop rickets.

But should no milk be available, nor powdered milk, yogurt or cheese either, it would still be possible to construct a nourishing diet. For instance, if peas and beans are combined with bread (for example, beans on toast, or pease pudding with fried bread), the mixture provides a protein blend on which children will grow.

An egg is valuable for children, not only on its own but even more when eaten together with bread (if scrambled or poached egg on toast had not already been invented the nutritional experts would certainly have invented them). And then meat, fish, chicken, liver, sausages, black pudding are more use, in the nutritional sense, to growing children than to their fathers.

But a shortage of milk does make it more difficult to supply the children with calcium for their bones. Without milk, the sort of fish of which the bones can be eaten would make a useful substitute. Sardines and salmon among the canned fish contain edible bones, as do whitebait and sprats. As we shall see, it is good practice to give infants cod-liver oil or some other source of vitamin D, either in the form of drops or capsules. For older children it would be sensible to continue with the vitamin if the time ever came when it was necessary to make a diet with little or no milk.

Vitamins for Youngsters

When grown-up people think about their own diets there is almost never any need for them to bother about vitamins. Things are, however, different for little children, and there are two reasons why this is so. The first is that, in proportion to their size – and in consequence in proportion to the amount of food they eat – little children need more vitamins than adults. The second reason is that because children are smaller than grown people, because they are active and because they are growing, it is easier for them to run out of one or other of the vitamins and suffer from a 'deficiency disease'.

VITAMIN FOR BONES

This is vitamin D. Sunshine can cause it to be produced in the child's skin. If, therefore, a child spends long hours tumbling about in the hot sun with not much on, there is no need to worry about vitamin D. But when the child lives in a cold, cloudy, rainy country (I name no names) and needs to be wrapped up against the weather or kept indoors, then it is a good idea to give a daily teaspoonful of cod-liver oil, or *a drop* (no more) of halibut-liver oil, or a vitamin D capsule until he is round about five years old. Later on butter and margarine, egg, cheese and milk can be depended upon to supply all the child needs.

VITAMIN A

Vitamin D preparations, like cod-liver oil, also supply vitamin A, so that if one of these is given there is no need to bother any more. But in the summer when there is no need to buy vitamin D, the careful parent needs to watch the vitamin A position. Butter, margarine, egg, cheese and milk supply this vitamin, liver is full of it, and greens and carrots supply their quota as well. So there is quite a wide variety of foods to choose from. If, therefore, you follow my repeated advice and provide a good mixture to your young children (as you should to yourself), vitamin A supplies should present no problem. The only possible difficulty comes if your child goes mad on one special 'favourite food' and raises a rumpus whenever you try to persuade him to be more sensible. Young children do develop these likes and dislikes and may go through phases when all they seem to want to eat is banana – or bacon. There is no need to worry unduly, nor, above all, to shout at the child that unless he finishes up his dinner he won't get any tea. Left to themselves and without too much harassment, children give up the fad of the day fairly quickly. If they see the rest of the family calmly getting on with *their* meals, they will probably soon settle down to eating anything that is offered. If, however, a fad goes on for more than a week or so, it may be prudent to make sure that the vitamin D concentrate that is being given also contains vitamin A.

VITAMIN C

This is the main virtue that children obtain from potatoes and from properly cooked greens and peas, and from apples, oranges and grapefruit. There should therefore be no difficulty in seeing that they get their vitamin C each day. It is also good practice to give them the summer fruits – cherries and raspberries, strawberries and plums – as they come in season each year. Tomatoes, of course, are fruit as well, and also supply vitamin C.

As well as the salad vegetables – lettuce, watercress and the like – greens and potatoes (particularly new potatoes) are really useful sources of vitamin C. Cooked vegetables, however, must not be cooked 'to death' or kept hot for ages before they are eaten. For young children vegetables and salads may present difficulties. They are fairly bulky and small children often don't like them (it may be quite rightly, bearing in mind their relatively big need for food compared with their relatively small stomachs). Whereas they do like fruit.

OTHER VITAMINS

The only reason why you should read this section is to protect yourself from being misled and confused by the superfluity of allegedly scientific advice which is sometimes pushed on to people who are responsible for bringing up young children.

A tremendous amount of study has been devoted to the complex and subtle ways in which children's bodies operate and in which children grow and change at the speed they do. All that most of us need to remember is, however, that thousands and thousands of happy, healthy children have been brought up by mothers who have no knowledge of science and only the haziest notion of what a vitamin might be.

I have written in some detail about vitamins A, C and D because there is just the possibility that young children may obtain less of one or other of these than they need if the mother does not know what to do about it. All the other twenty or more known vitamins are of no importance to a practical mother because in ordinary circumstances in a western country little children *always* get enough of them so long as they are given enough to eat.

Children Are Sometimes Right

It is interesting to look back and consider all those strict rules of diet that parents used to impose on children on the grounds that this or that was 'good for them'. Nowadays many of these rules (not all, but many) can be seen to be nonsense.

For instance, it is nonsense that *eating between meals* is always bad. For young children particularly, eating between meals is almost essential if they are to grow well and be healthy, as long as their snacks are sensibly chosen. Whereas his mother may enjoy a cup of tea for her elevenses, the five-year-old can usefully put away a glass of milk and a slice of cake, or a piece of cheese on a biscuit, as well. And the same holds for his mid-afternoon snack.

Parents used at one time to deplore their children's liking for *ice-cream* and stop them from eating it. Now it is realised that even if it contains vegetable fats rather than cream, it has milk in it and can make a useful contribution to a child's diet.

Today it is fashionable to decry *breakfast cereals*. In fact, children are quite right to like them. They are sweet and tasty, and they stoke the child up with the energy-value which he needs first thing in the morning. Furthermore, they make a good vehicle for milk which is, of course, of more use to young children than to the rest of us. About the only thing to be said against breakfast cereals would be that they might be considered poor value for money. Before deciding whether this is so or not, you should consider whether the lower cost of bread and milk or perhaps porridge (both of which are about equivalent to breakfast cereal in nutritional value) would be balanced by the trouble of getting the children to eat them. Perhaps it's worth a try!

Nor should the children's liking for *sweetness* be dismissed out of hand. Sugar is a concentrated source of the energy-value they need. Of course, they shouldn't be given too much sugar; it will make them fat. But left to themselves, young children are unlikely to eat over-much sugar. Given a chance, they will go for eggs and bacon, or fish and chips. Sweets themselves, however, are a different matter. It is easy to over-indulge children and to pop sweets into their mouths at all times of day just to keep them quiet. But two kinds of harm are being done. Firstly, the sugar constantly in their mouths will encourage the bacteria that are always present in saliva to attack their teeth, especially if they are not made to clean their teeth, or at least rinse their mouths out with water, after eating sweets. In addition, there are surely better ways than bribery of ensuring good behaviour.

Most young children have a liking for *white bread*, even though some well-meaning parents hold an almost religious faith in the nutritional virtues of brown bread. It would be curious if the children should be proved to have been sensible after all. The argument that brown bread contains more vitamins than white bread is quite irrelevant: the difference in vitamin content is not very great and nearly all children get all the bread-vitamins they need anyway. A second argument in favour of brown bread is that it contains more fibre than white bread, but the evidence that fibre is especially beneficial to health and nutrition is not very strong and indeed there is a possibility that fibre may not be a good thing for young children. If this possibility should one day be confirmed, children's liking for white bread would be proved to have been justified.

Not very long ago, it was discovered that small amounts of the metal zinc are necessary for healthy growth and development. Without sufficient zinc, children grow more slowly and do not grow as tall as they should. But because an ordinary mixed diet provides as much zinc as anybody needs, I have said nothing about zinc up till now. New evidence is coming to light, however, about the relation between zinc and fibre.

If you write in ink on a piece of paper, the dye in the ink stays stuck on the paper. It does not rub off or, if it is first allowed to dry, wash off either. The reason is that the fibres of the paper form what is virtually a chemical bond with the dye. These fibres are quite similar to the fibre, or roughage, in brown bread. It now appears that they also latch on to zinc. The zinc becomes so firmly fixed that it remains attached to the fibres as they pass all the way through the digestive system, into the bowels, and so out of the body altogether.

In the light of all this, it is interesting that round about 1870 it was noticed by doctors that the heights and weights of boys and girls from poorer families were beginning to increase so that, year by year they approached more and more closely to those of children from richer and more fortunate homes. At the same time, just about this date of 1870, new techniques were introduced into the milling industry which for the first time brought white flour and white bread within the reach of people for whom previously they had been too expensive. Cause-and-effect relationships are never easy to define precisely, but the fact remains that during the time when the fibre content of the nation's diet began progressively to decrease, an improvement became noticeable in the stature of young children, starting at the earlier ages. The reduction in fibre is now considered to have resulted in zinc becoming more readily available to growing children. Of course, should the advocates of brown bread and the virtues of fibre prove to be correct, the disadvantage which fibre has in tying up zinc could be overcome by the public-health authorities adding extra zinc to fibre-containing foods. Meanwhile, however, we ought to give those children who like white bread the credit for having chosen what in fact may be the best thing for them.

Don't worry about zinc. There is always a danger that research scientists, over-eager to publicise their own particular field of interest, may thereby confuse people who only want to know how best to feed themselves and their children. The discovery that zinc is of any importance in the diet is a case in point. For normal healthy adults, the new discoveries about zinc are of no practical interest whatever because zinc is quite common and no matter how eccentrically they chose their meals they are almost certain to obtain all the zinc they need or more. However, you might be interested to know that good sources of zinc include meat of all kinds, and peas and beans (so beans on toast comes up trumps again). There is little zinc in greens or fruit.

Nutrition and Happiness

'Better is a dinner of herbs where love is, than a stalled ox and hatred therewith', says the Book of Proverbs in the Bible, and this is scientifically true in terms of nutrition. It is particularly true for children. Observations of young children (and also, incidentally, trials with young cattle and young rats) clearly show that if two groups of youngsters are given the same ration, the group who eat their meals happy in the company of people they trust and love thrive better than those compelled to eat in chilly 'institutional' surroundings. All this only confirms what wise parents – and the writer of the Book of Proverbs – already knew very well. The moral is clear and can be set down as a number of rules of nutrition which are far more important than much of the stuff that is put about concerning wholemeal bread, honey, roughage and half a dozen other fashionable fads.

☐ If you feel you must scold your children and make them miserable, whether 'for their own good' or merely to relieve your own feelings, *don't scold at mealtimes*.

☐ Take steps to make the children's meals agreeable and peaceful events. If possible, gather the whole family round the table to eat meals together in a hum of cheerful conversation.

☐ It follows that small children should be taught something of good order and good manners at the table. Otherwise the aim of good-humoured happiness – the 'X vitamin' for good nutrition – will be frustrated for the whole family.

As Wordsworth says, 'the child is father of the man'. It is

in these early years that habits are formed and that children drink in knowledge: knowledge about how to walk about and play, how to draw, paint and build models, how to recognise what is good to eat and what is not. And they also learn about people and how they behave. If parents are weak in enforcing rules, have double standards – that is, say one thing and do another – if they are quarrelsome, noisy and cruel (yes, there are parents who are cruel, both in the things they say and in the unfeeling things they do) – and all these can be clearly observed at the dinner-table – children will learn these things too.

Babies

'Nowadays a woman may have many parts to play:
she may be a Prime Minister . . .'

A NEW-BORN BABY can live for a while on its body stores without eating anything. It is often two or three days after the birth before a mother is able to establish a sufficient milk supply, and this delay will normally do the baby no harm. Thereafter, the baby should live for the next twelve weeks or so almost solely on milk.

Milk for Babies

It is a great advantage to a baby to start life on its mother's milk. Mothers who breast-feed their babies are in a good position to show them affection; love and tenderness and a quiet place are important factors in babies' nutrition.

Furthermore, the milk with which a mother supplies her baby is ideally suited to his needs. Not all milk has the same make-up: there are striking differences in the chemical compositions of human milk and cows' milk. Calves, for which cows' milk is really intended, grow to adult size in two years compared with the sixteen to eighteen years a baby takes; and cows' milk contains much more protein than human milk does – 3.5 per cent compared with 1.5 per cent in human milk. On the other hand, the amount of sugar in human milk (6.8 per cent) is greater than the 5.0 per cent in cows' milk. Cows' milk as delivered by the milkman, therefore, however nourishing and however well it suits little calves, is not precisely what a baby needs, and its composition must be altered (by adding sugar and water) before it is given to infants.

Finally, breast milk has the great advantage of coming to the baby uncontaminated and at the right temperature.

BABIES ARE SPECIAL

A baby needs the same nutrients as anybody else.

However, a mother must pay closer attention to the details of feeding a baby than to the nutrition of herself, her husband or the older children. One reason is that, once they get going, babies grow more quickly than at any other time in their lives. To do this they need all the various components that make up the bones and muscles they have to produce. At the same time they are small, they have no teeth and they are new to the business of living. Moreover, a baby cannot speak. This means that he is unable to tell those around him that he is hungry and – more important – when he is thirsty. The first and most important factor in a baby's nutrition is to ensure that he has enough to eat.

Getting Enough to Eat

Babies, like people, are all different. Some need more to eat than others do. However, the generally accepted amounts of breast milk required by a baby whose weight at birth was around 7 lb is shown below. Big babies usually need a little more and small babies a little less; even so, individuals may vary.

Age in days	Amount of milk required daily
3	5 oz
4	$7\frac{1}{2}$ oz
5	10 oz
6	$12\frac{1}{2}$ oz
7	15 oz
8–14	2 oz per lb of baby

From the third week onwards, a baby needs about $2\frac{1}{2}$ oz of milk per pound of its body weight every day: for instance, a 10-lb baby will need about 25 oz of milk daily. You can find out whether a breast-fed baby is getting about the amount he needs by test-weighing him before and after each feed, and in the first few days of life this can be useful because during this period most babies lose weight however much milk they take in. (On average, a baby loses about six ounces in weight by the fourth day of his life, although small babies generally lose less and big babies more, up to as much as one pound; this loss is usually replaced quickly, and the baby is as a rule back to his birth weight by the time he is eight or nine days old.) Once growth is established and he is beginning to thrive, his increase in weight week by week is a fair indication that he is getting enough to eat.

Because of a baby's urgent nutritional needs on the one hand and his small stomach on the other he must be provided with a programme of feeds. Most babies settle down fairly quickly to having five feeds each day, usually though not necessarily given at 6 a.m., 10 a.m., 2 p.m., 6 p.m. and 10 p.m. Very small babies, or strong hungry babies that cry for their meals, may be given six feeds a day, however, at least to start with. By dividing his food up like this into a series of 'meals', the baby is able to get enough to eat, and by the time he weighs 14 or 15 lb he will be consuming 35–37 oz of milk a day.

Breast or Bottle?

For all God's creatures – and that includes babies as well as you and me – food provides at least three things. Firstly, it supplies what engineers talking about a machine or a factory would describe as 'chemical inputs'. Secondly, it gives pleasure by its taste, smell, look, feel and (with crunchy foods) sound; and, thirdly, it binds us in happiness to our parents, our family, our friends and – at the Lord Mayor's banquet or the dinner of the bowls club – to the community to which we belong. Each of these three factors has a bearing on the question: is breast-feeding better nutrition than bottle-feeding?

THE THRIVING BABY

From the point of view of providing a baby with enough food and with the proper kind of food, there is not a penny to choose between breast-feeding and bottle-feeding. Fashions change: people become as irrational and emotional about breast-feeding as they do about politics, religion or their favourite football team, and come to hold strong views about breast-feeding even though such views may change as time passes. The fact remains, however, that two generations of infants in the advanced industrialised countries of the world have been brought up on bottle-feeding mixtures to become perfectly normal, healthy grown-up citizens. There is no strong evidence to show whether or not there are more badly nourished babies brought up on the bottle than there are on the breast.

THE CONTENTED BABY

From the baby's point of view breast-feeding serves two functions. It provides the nutrition upon which his physical health, his growth and his well-being depend. At the same time, it is an act of love. While the child is in his mother's womb, his reactions are entirely self-centred: he takes what he needs from his mother's bloodstream regardless of her own requirements. And when he is born, the baby is aware at first only of himself and his own needs. It is remarkable, however, how soon he becomes conscious of the world around him; of all the people in the world, his mother is the most important, not only as the main source of food and comfort but also of love. Breast-feeding can be a potent lesson – the first and perhaps the most important lesson in life – of the well-being that comes from being loved and from loving.

ONE OF THE FAMILY

Some people nowadays talk and argue as if babies who are

not breast-fed were going to be handicapped for life, and as if mothers who choose not to breast-feed their babies must be a mixture of the wicked witch of Endor and Cinderella's two cruel ugly sisters all wrapped up in one. But the nutrients an infant needs can be provided equally well either by bottle-feeding or by breast-feeding; and although a breast-fed baby can be cuddled and loved in a particularly direct way, many, many mothers can find ways to express their love for their babies while bottle-feeding them. Moreover, if breast-feeding a child would disrupt the mother's own life and the harmony of her family, the baby's welfare will be better served by bottle-feeding.

A woman is no more a mere instrument for feeding a baby than a man is a mere agent for propagating one. Nowadays a woman may have many parts to play: she may be a Prime Minister or a doctor, the head of a business or the main breadwinner of a family. Even when social arrangements are such that she is provided with help and financial support when her baby is born and during its first months of life, she should be free to choose whether she *wants* to give up her daily avocation to take care of a baby.

All these considerations have a bearing on the question of whether the nutrition of a particular baby is better served by his being breast-fed or bottle-fed. An infant, like every other individual, is not an isolated entity and in real life his nutritional status cannot be considered merely as a matter of food chemistry.

Vitamins for Babies

Babies, again like everyone else, need vitamins. Unlike other people, however, it *is* quite important for those responsible for feeding them to take trouble to see that they get the vitamins they need.

Negligible vitamins

In rich industrial countries vitamin A, vitamin E and the

half-dozen or more B-vitamins simply are not worth worrying over, always assuming, firstly, that the baby's mother was properly looked after and well fed before the baby was born, and that, secondly, the baby is consuming an adequate amount of milk, either from his mother or from a bottle. (In poorer parts of the world, of course, this assumption cannot be made so easily, and babies' diets may well need careful supplementation.)

Essential vitamins

Vitamin D. Babies grow quickly and their bones grow too. Unless they receive enough vitamin D or are out in the sun most of the day, they may develop an unpleasant disease called rickets; and the quicker they grow, the more likely they are to suffer from the disease. It is, therefore, good practice to make sure that the baby gets a daily drop of vitamin D concentrate or a teaspoonful of cod-liver oil.

Vitamin C. A well-fed mother who drinks orange juice, eats fresh vegetables or takes vitamin C tablets will give her baby all the vitamin C he needs in her breast milk. A mother bottle-feeding her baby should make sure that the food formula contains vitamin C (also called 'ascorbic acid'); if it does not, she should give the baby a daily spoonful of orange juice or rose-hip syrup if he can tolerate it, or a drop of vitamin C concentrate.

Vitamin K. A very few new-born babies have a tendency to bleeding which is caused by a shortage of vitamin K. Some scientists, particularly in the United States, suggest that one injection of vitamin K when the baby is born is a prudent precaution. But this is a decision which may safely be left in the doctors' hands: mothers do not need to bother about it at all.

Bottle-feeding

The people who put together the baby-food preparations do so by combining appropriate amounts of cows' milk, sugar and water and evaporating the mixture so as to produce a powder which will recombine easily with water when it is prepared for use. The reconstituted mixture should contain almost exactly the same proportions of protein, fat and sugar that human milk does. The amounts of salt and some of the other mineral ingredients may be rather different but on the whole the match is quite accurate.

This match can, however, be achieved only *if you follow exactly* the instructions for making up the feed.

If the instructions call for a *level* scoopful, don't put in a heaped scoopful or the feed will be too concentrated and the baby will be thirsty afterwards. (*Never* put in an extra scoopful for luck!)

If the instructions call for a *heaped* scoopful, don't make up a feed using level measures. Should you do so the baby may not get enough to eat.

As far as the size of feeds and the feeding programme are concerned, the system of bottle-feeding is much the same as that for breast-feeding. With bottle-feeding, however, it is essential to make sure that the bottle, the teat and any utensils involved are all kept scrupulously clean, either by boiling them for at least five minutes or by using a proprietary preparation such as Milton, according to the directions on the label. At one time it was considered important to ensure that the feed was warmed exactly to blood-heat before being given to the baby. Many American experts, coming from the land of the ice-cream, now consider that it does not matter to the baby if his feed is given cold. Not all babies agree with them, however.

BOTTLE-FEEDING MIXTURE

If a child is to be bottle-fed, there are advantages in buying a ready-prepared powdered mixture from a welfare clinic or chemist's shop. Such mixtures contain an appropriate balance of protein and sugar and perhaps also supplementary vitamins, and great attention is paid during their manufacturing and packaging to ensuring that they are free from harmful bacteria.

Should prepared bottle-feeding mixtures not be available, however, you can yourself make up satisfactory combinations of protein, carbohydrate and fat, substantially similar to breast milk.

Note: Always wash your hands scrupulously before starting operations and take great care to sterilise all the utensils employed, as well as the bottles and the teats.

For babies during the first weeks of life: Use a mixture of 10 oz of water, 10 oz of pasteurised or homogenised milk and 1 oz of sugar (these quantities will make up roughly one day's supply).

For babies from two to three weeks old: Use 7 oz of water, 14 oz of pasteurised or homogenised milk and 1 oz of sugar.

For babies three months old and upwards: Use 7 oz of water, 21 oz of pasteurised or homogenised milk and 1 oz of sugar. Alternatively use 17 oz of water, 11 oz of evaporated milk and 1 oz of sugar.

To prepare the feeds: Boil the water in a saucepan, and add the milk. Bring the mixture back to the boil, stirring meanwhile, and boil it for five minutes. Add the sugar, stir, and pour the mixture into sterilised feeding-bottles. Put on the teats, cool the bottles as quickly as possible, and store them in the refrigerator until they are needed.

Don't Forget Water

From 60 to 65 per cent of an adult's body consists of water.

A baby has a higher proportion of water in his make-up – between 70 and 75 per cent. It may happen, particularly at the beginning of life when a baby tends to lose weight, that he can become short of water. It is, therefore, good practice to give water to drink so that the baby can slake his thirst without perforce having to 'eat' at the same time.

Later on when the infant is growing steadily it is still important to ensure that he has enough water to drink. Since bottle-feeding mixtures are saltier than breast milk, bottle feeds may leave the baby feeling thirsty, even though they are in liquid form. It may still therefore be useful to offer the baby drinks of water. Never add any extra salt to the bottle feed just because it may seem insipid and flavourless to an adult's taste. Too much salt can be harmful to a young baby, and he is unlikely to find the unsalted feed unattractive, whatever you may think of it.

Now For Mixed Feeding

Milk is ideal to feed young babies on, but regardless of popular belief, *it is not a perfect food*. In particular, it contains very little iron. For the first few weeks of his life the baby keeps himself going by using the iron supplies he has in his body when he is born. While it is important not to keep him too long on a diet made up entirely of milk, whether it be breast milk or the milk-and-sugar mixtures of which artificial baby foods are mainly composed, milk will be enough for him for the first three or four months of his life, though some people suggest that some solid food is needed as early as three to six weeks of age.

FIRST FOODS

Fruit and fruit-juice. A little fruit-juice added to the baby's drinking water is a good way to start mixed feeding. Cooked fruit made into a purée and strained is useful. Ripe banana mushed up and given with a spoon is popular.

These all add iron and minerals which milk does not provide.

Vegetables. Almost any vegetable, including tomatoes, carefully cooked and sieved, will also contribute iron, other minerals and vitamins A and C.

Egg yolk. Usually given from a soft-boiled egg, or hard-boiled and worked into a paste, egg yolk is a particularly good source of iron.

Cereal. Cereal supplies fuel-value as well as minerals, and also provides its contribution of iron. It will be particularly welcomed by the baby with a good appetite.

By the time the baby is six months old he will be quite accustomed to a variety of foods in addition to his milk feed. Gradually, therefore, as the eighth month approaches, the food the baby eats approximates more and more closely to that of his older brothers and sisters. Sample meals for babies of this age might be as follows:

The first meal (when the baby wakes in the morning) will be 6–8 oz of breast milk or bottle feed;

The second meal (at 10 a.m.) will comprise in addition egg yolk and toast, rusk and butter, and cereal;

The third meal (at 2 p.m.) will include sieved vegetables, egg, perhaps fish or even a little meat broth, custard or junket and stewed apple;

The fourth meal (at 4.30 p.m.) will comprise a thin honey or jam sandwich, or a sponge finger;

The fifth meal (at 6.30 p.m.) and the sixth (at 10.30 p.m.) will each consist of 6–8 oz of milk feed.

Fat Babies and Thin Babies

Although new-born infants have special nutritional needs of their own, as they grow their requirements gradually approach those of everybody else. And the best way to ensure that their diet is satisfactory is – as for everyone else – to make sure that they are given a variety of food. There are, of course, special considerations for babies. But the most important responsibilities which a mother faces in feeding her baby are to make sure that *he gets enough to eat* and to make sure that *he does not eat too much.*

UNDERFED BABIES

There should be no need to tell a mother that all babies are different. They come in all shapes and sizes, and some as they grow are consistently bigger than others. Sensible mothers (those who have not read too many books about nutrition!) know that some babies *eat more* than others and that some babies *need more* than others.

A baby's appetite is some indication of the amount of food he needs. It is not a certain guide, however. Babies cannot talk to their mothers to tell them when they are hungry; a breast-fed baby may find it difficult to obtain as much milk as he wants; some babies are sleepy at feed-time and need encouragement; finally, there may be some outside reason why the baby is distracted from taking as much food as he needs. If you are wondering whether your baby is getting enough to eat, then check to make sure that his weight is steadily increasing from week to week, and take a good look to make sure that he is thriving.

Is he having enough to eat? A baby should be rounded and plump all over. It is true that obesity can be a danger. But don't be led astray by fashionable talk about 'slimming' into starving your child.

Some mothers try to deceive themselves when their baby fails to grow by pretending that he is 'wiry'. Babies vary in shape (just as grown people do) but they ought not to be wiry.

Do not try to judge whether a baby is underfed by looking only at his face. When the baby's face tells you that he has been underfed (which it does when he comes to look, not like a baby at all, but like an old man) things have become really serious.

A well-fed baby is easily recognised. His skin is smooth and supple and, if gently pinched, is elastic and springy, and his muscles feel firm, compact and strong. In addition, he steadily gains weight from week to week. The baby that is getting too little to eat, on the other hand, will be restless and cry a good deal. He will not be gaining weight consistently, and his muscles will be flabby rather than firm. He may tend to lose fat, first from the inside of his thighs, then from his buttocks, and after that from his belly and chest. His face becomes wasted last of all.

If a breast-fed baby shows some of these signs of underfeeding, then there is probably need for supplementary bottle-feeding, or the introduction of feeds of cereal or other appropriate solid foods.

OVERFED BABIES

Just as there are tall slender adults who never have to trouble about putting on weight, so are there babies who are unlikely to become really fat. On the other hand, there are men and women of squarer build who, if they overeat, are very likely to become obese. And of these, those most likely to become fat men and women are the ones who have been fat babies. The commonest cause of obesity in babies is a mother who makes up the bottle-feed mixture too strong, perhaps by adding an extra spoonful of powdered milk 'for luck', or by putting in heaped scoopfuls when the recipe calls for level scoopfuls.

Another way to produce a fat baby is to give too many pieces of cake, sugary biscuit, cereal or fingers of bread and butter, *in addition* to the recommended bottle feeds, or to start such extra feeding too soon. Some mothers believe that, so far as their babies are concerned, 'the bigger the better'; they also seem to think that the quicker the baby grows the healthier he is. Both these ideas are mistaken; moreover, an obese baby, even if he gets thin again when he grows into an older child, is likely to have a weight problem as an adult (and when I write 'he' I mean, as usual, girls as well as boys). There is also some evidence implying that if a baby has been overfed so as to grow too fat and too fast, then he may not live as long as he might otherwise have done.

Is he getting too fat? Firstly, the fat baby is too big for his age. In assessing whether this is so, it is obviously important to take into account whether his father and mother are big or small people. Secondly, while babies' faces ought to be plump a fat baby's face is so fat that his features appear to be small. He often has a double chin. His breasts may appear to bulge, and if he is *very* fat his stomach may look distended and pendulous.

Clearly, a baby that is growing too fat must be given less to eat. The most direct way of reducing food supply is to cut down the quantity of each of the feeds or to space them out at longer intervals, or even to drop one feed altogether. But it may be supplementary feeding that is making a baby too fat: either too much solid food may be being provided, or the choice of what is given may be wrong. Cereals, sugar, bread and butter, cakes and biscuits are more 'fattening' (that is to say, they possess a higher energy-value) than sieved vegetables and fruit. Although it is a good idea gradually to introduce a baby to the foods that the rest of the family eats, it is best not to give too much of the 'easy' items like fingers of bread and jam or buttered scone, rather than the more troublesome things such as vegetables, meat or fish which have to be specially prepared by being cut up small or minced.

Remember, too, that fatness in a baby, as in anybody else, is related partly to the amount he eats and partly to the amount of exercise he takes. A baby needs exercise and must be given the opportunity to kick about and use his limbs. He will get fatter than ever if he is kept too much in his cot or pram without having the chance now and then to struggle about on the floor.

Fads and Fancies

After the first three or four months of his life, a baby obtains his nourishment from a mixture of foods, just as the rest of the family does. But a mother may sometimes worry. She reads, for example, that egg or cheese are good for babies. Yet her baby spits them out, and only goes for mashed-up banana. There are two things worth saying about likes and dislikes.

ALL IN THE FAMILY

The baby begins very early to obtain love and companionship, and soon picks up the idea that there is at least one other person in the world besides himself and that life is a happier and more satisfactory experience because this is so. Quite soon he also benefits from learning to enjoy being a part of the family and learning to behave properly as such. And encouraging him to learn these lessons is an important part of caring for him. Don't, therefore, make a great fuss if your baby refuses yogurt or stewed apple or whatever his current aversion may be. Obviously, you must see that he does not seriously underfeed himself, and there is almost always a medical reason if he does. But *there is no need to attempt to make every meal a perfect mixture of all the vitamins, proteins and minerals there are*. Good nutrition requires simply that a proper mixture is consumed over a reasonable period of time, say a week. Good baby care requires, too, that family relationships are happily established and maintained.

BABIES AREN'T FOOLS

There have been some interesting experiments in which babies and toddlers have been given the opportunity to choose their own diet. They have been faced with twenty or thirty dishes containing a variety of different foods: banana, apples, strawberries, minced chicken, fish, cheese, rice pudding, sponge cake and so forth. Taken over the whole period of the trial, the children chose a pretty good diet, although some babies from time to time went on a 'jag' and ate one item – banana, perhaps – for days on end. However, when no one interfered with them they soon gave this up and began to choose a mixture of other foods that set the balance straight.

Obviously, this experiment was carefully supervised. Although a wide choice of food was offered, there was nothing that would harm the infants even if they did indulge themselves to excess. Nor were all the foods full of sugar; the children were thus free to choose, if they wished, a diet *not* containing sugar. Besides which, milk and milk mixtures, cheese, egg, meat and poultry were available. The moral is that, left to themselves, young children will normally *like what is good for them*, so there is no need to fuss.

Feeding and Loving

The feeding of a baby illustrates especially vividly all the problems facing people who want to use nutritional science sensibly.

Babies are tough. This is one aspect of the truth. Babies *are* quite tough and they are adaptable as well. I could provide you with a table of your baby's requirements of calories, grams, milligrams and micrograms of this, that and the other; nevertheless, provided general principles are adhered to, he will thrive without your bothering about tables, and will emerge as a well-fed child.

Babies are tender. On the other hand, whereas an adult can eat a nutritionally *terrible* diet (of bread and water or, dismasted at sea, of baked beans and gin) for quite a long time without coming to serious harm, a baby wrongly fed may be quickly damaged.

Babies are individuals. This means that each one needs to be closely watched : to see that he is well and happy, putting on weight and with firm elastic flesh. One baby may sleep more than another, one may feed more voraciously but all babies need to grow and progress steadily week by week.

Babies are part of the family. Nutrition is the science underlying eating; eating is the basis of meals, but meals are also social occasions. This implies, in all scientific seriousness, that happiness has something to do with health. Love, too, is thus concerned with good nutrition as well.

To produce the well-nourished baby, one necessary ingredient is watchful, well-informed love.

Eating for Two

'You should remember, however, that your baby
shares your bloodstream ...'

IF YOU ARE, or if you propose to become, pregnant, then you are going to be given a good deal of assorted advice. Here is some more, about how to become a well-fed expectant mother. This aim is not too difficult of achievement, however, provided that you pay attention to the rules of nutrition and the special ways in which they apply to you during your pregnancy.

Before You Are Pregnant

WHEN DIET DOESN'T MATTER

Food and nutrition have almost nothing to do with becoming pregnant. In spite of some remarkably persistent and even bizarre traditions, there is no such thing as a 'food for love'. Even where serious malnutrition is rife, the birth-rate is often high – frequently higher than in more prosperous societies – while on the other hand overfed women and their gluttonous husbands have no particular difficulties in starting families. The reason for the low birth-rate of rich countries is not the plentiful food their inhabitants enjoy, but rather that prosperous people generally choose to have small families. Of course, if underfeeding is so severe and prolonged that people are starving they will become incapable of producing children.

WHEN DIET IS IMPORTANT

A baby in his mother's womb is a voracious creature, who seizes from his mother's blood the various components he requires for his own development: calcium for his bones, protein for his flesh and all the other necessary nutrients. This is why thin, drawn, undernourished women can produce large, well-formed babies. But they only do this at a cost to themselves: such women lose their looks, their teeth and their health when they have their children. In her own interests, therefore, a young woman ought to feed herself properly *before* she is called upon to 'eat for two'.

But a potential mother should also be well-nourished so that when she does become pregnant her child will develop properly before the time comes for him to be born. In the first few weeks of a baby's life he depends for the iron and some of the vitamins he needs on the stores he brought with him into the world. And these he must have been able to get from his mother. But he cannot get what he needs if it is not there to take. A woman well-nourished before her child is conceived is better able to give him a good start in life. After all, no matter how carefully she manages her diet when she is pregnant, nine months is not a long time to put right what may have been neglected or mismanaged for years.

Finally, good nutrition is important to an expectant mother because women who were well-fed as girls have less trouble bearing their children than those who ate only a poor and unsatisfactory diet. In particular, a girl who has had rickets, as a result of her having had too little vitamin D in her food or too little sunshine when *she* was a child, may have a particularly difficult labour if the disease has affected the shape of her pelvis.

The First Three Months

During these three months you need to eat a diet no different from what any sensible healthy woman eats, pregnant or not. But although the little foetus does not at this stage make any demands that you cannot take in your stride, you are aware of his presence and conscious that you want to give him the best possible chance when he at last comes into the world; and this gives you a useful opportunity about your own diet.

Have you been allowing yourself to become fat? If so,

this is your last chance for several months to do something about it. A bit more exercise and rather less chocolate cake could make all the difference. Fat women can produce healthy babies, to be sure, but they do tend to produce fat babies who may in their turn have what we politely call 'weight problems' when *they* grow up. On the other hand, have you been too busy, hard at it at work, rushing home to get dressed, perhaps out dancing every night, or at home worrying and not eating properly? If so, you may have become overtired and – to be blunt – underfed. Here, then, are three precious months to do something about this too: to rest more, and to eat more and better meals.

While putting quantity right, it is a good thing to check that the quality is right as well. Having a cooked meal most days, whether at midday or in the evening, makes it easy to ensure that the week's menus include vegetables: greens, potatoes, green peas, runner beans and all the rest. Remember that the best way to make sure that the quality *is* right, and that all those varied proteins, vitamins and minerals are properly represented, is to take thought of variety – and eat it. Jog your memory by going down to the market to see what has come into season recently. Suddenly you will remember how long it is since you last ate Brussels sprouts; and at the butcher's it may come to mind that you have not eaten liver (or heart, kidney or brains, maybe) since you were at school. It is not that these articles, any more than cheese or mackerel, possess any magical nutritional properties. It is just that they help you to follow the second principle of good nutrition – to eat a variety of different foods.

NOW FOR A WARNING

There is another reason for you to be careful about what you put into your mouth at this time. Early in his existence, your baby is particularly sensitive to outside influences. You probably know that it is very dangerous to catch

German measles during the first three months of pregnancy. The disease itself is trivial but the effect on the unborn child may be disastrous. Similarly, it was discovered all too tragically that taking an excellent tranquilliser, thalidomide, early in pregnancy (when some women feel themselves to be in particular need of a tranquilliser) caused terrible deformities in children. Even smoking may adversely affect the foetus at this early stage (later in pregnancy it certainly does so: heavy smokers tend to have rather small babies).

The effects of German measles and thalidomide illustrate how important it is to the baby's safety to stick to these general principles during the early months of pregnancy:

do not take any unnecessary drugs, not even aspirin and certainly not tranquillisers or sleeping pills;

do not smoke;

put your diet right if it was wrong before.

Six Months Before D-Day

Everything your baby is, when he is born, he must have obtained from you, his mother. And all his body's constituents – the calcium for his skull and bones, the protein for his flesh, the iron that is stored away in his liver and so forth – these and much more must be supplied from the food you eat. And this must be *extra* to that which you need for your own health.

MORE TO EAT

During these months, you need to eat about 10 per cent more food than usual: 10 per cent more calories, that is, and 10 per cent more protein, too. Although it is better not to be overweight when you start your pregnancy, it is equally important for a slimming fanatic, who spends her life worrying whether or not every mouthful of food she eats is fattening, not to carry her preoccupation to extremes during the last six months of her pregnancy.

CALCIUM

Besides this extra need for food in general during the later months of pregnancy, your need for calcium is more than doubled. Your unborn child will ruthlessly take calcium from your system even though this may mean that you lose the calcium you need for your teeth; before this was realised, no effort was made to see that pregnant women had plenty of calcium in their food and 'for every child a tooth' was the cost most women paid for ignorance.

Extra protein certainly and extra calcium probably can be obtained by drinking plenty of milk and it is a good idea to do so, if you like milk and can afford to buy it. Cheese and powdered milk, sardines and canned salmon (providing you eat the bones) are also useful sources of calcium. Just the same, your needs for calcium are so great, particularly during the last three months of pregnancy, that it is probably sensible to take calcium tablets as an insurance.

IRON

During these important months, your daily need for iron is up by at least 25 per cent. This is partly to supply the day-to-day needs of the developing foetus, and partly to build up a reserve for him to take with him in his liver. The extra iron is also important to you yourself, to make good the losses that will come when the baby is born. The amount of blood you will lose then is probably more than you would have lost in menstruation had you not been pregnant, and in addition a further loss in the afterbirth has to be made good. Besides which you will also have to provide for the small but significant amount of iron you will give in your breast milk.

Quite a number of women live on the verge of anaemia without knowing it. These are the women who are likely to become seriously anaemic – breathless, tired and generally 'below par' – during the last six months of their pregnancy unless they do something about it. And the first thing to do is to peg away at eating meat, which is one of the best ways of obtaining iron. There is no need to spend a fortune on prime steak; mince is just as good. Black pudding is best of all, and liver runs it a close second. But you can obtain the extra iron you need, if not so agreeably, certain at lower cost by taking iron tablets, which your doctor or clinic will probably give you.

VITAMINS

During the last six months of your pregnancy you probably need twice as much vitamin C as usual. This means that you should eat plenty of oranges and grapefruit and – especially if it is summertime – other fresh fruit as well. Don't spend a fortune if prices are high, but do remember that strawberries and raspberries, gooseberries and blackcurrants all contain useful amounts of vitamin C.

Tomatoes, lettuce and watercress are good, too, and so are cabbage, cauliflower, Brussels sprouts and broccoli. Be careful, though, when you cook them to chop the cabbage or green vegetables into the briskly boiling water (don't put the greens into cold water and then bring it to the boil) and also, as soon as the greens are cooked, eat them (don't put them into the oven to keep them hot).

Usually I advise people not to worry over this, that or the other vitamin or horrifying visions of the harm that will come from eating almost any food you care to name (if you believe everything that is published in the papers). If they keep to the simple rules for sensible eating, all the complexities of nutritional science will come out right. During pregnancy, however, it *is* useful to think about one vitamin, at least, as something to be careful about and not as something that turns up automatically in a sensible mixture of wholesome food. This is vitamin D.

Most grown people need not bother about vitamin D. There is some in milk, butter and eggs and in such fish as herrings and, besides, you can pick up vitamin D from the sunshine (when there is any) that shines on your skin. Vitamin D is particularly connected with the formation of bones, the skull and, in due course, teeth. Obviously, when you are not pregnant vitamin D has no special interest for you. Your bones and skull are fully formed and you have finished producing the two sets of teeth that are all you are ever going to have. But once your pregnancy is well established, everything changes. The foundations of the baby's skull and all his bones are being laid down: in fact, at this time you require four times the amount of vitamin D you normally need, and it is therefore sensible for you to take vitamin D capsules in addition to your diet.

In spite of what elegant young ladies in bikinis may believe, sunbathing at the seaside confers virtually no nutritional benefits to most adults. Indeed, the only time in a young woman's life when sunbathing would be of positive nutritional benefit is likely to be the one time when she may *not* want young men to eye her exposed and lightly oiled body – namely, when she is in the later stages of pregnancy.

Nuisances of Pregnancy

MORNING SICKNESS

Morning sickness, like seasickness, is disagreeable, a nuisance and – as all sufferers from either disability inevitably feel – *unfair*. It is unfair because some people have it and some inexplicably don't. There are great, big, strapping, no-nonsense girls who suffer miserably. Poor, pathetic, apprehensive little women, constantly complaining about their nerves, may sail through their pregnancies unscathed. Like seasickness, too, morning sickness, though troublesome, is not serious for most women, amounting to no more than a feeling of nausea in the early morning during the first few weeks of pregnancy. This, unpleasant though it may be, soon passes off and, as pregnancy proceeds, there is a good chance that you come to feel better than you did before you were pregnant.

For some women, however, morning sickness involves what its name implies – being sick. And a few particularly unlucky women may vomit so much, and not merely in the morning but all day, that they are ill. The loss of liquid from the body can become so serious that the unfortunate sufferer may become gravely distressed, and even have to be packed off to hospital. When this is done, the problem usually quickly solves itself.

As far as scientific investigation can tell us, nutrition has nothing to do with morning sickness. Moreover, scientific research has so far failed to discover *what* causes morning sickness. And I have to admit that scientists have turned up no useful information on how best to treat it. There are dozens of old wives' remedies purporting to prevent it from happening or to treat it once it begins. Since it is an affliction of the early weeks of pregnancy only, almost any 'cure' can claim to be effective if you persevere with it long enough. It does seem helpful to have a little something to eat before you get up in the morning. Breakfast in bed is not a bad idea, if there is someone who is willing to bring it.

The best advice that can be given you, therefore, if you are a sufferer from morning sickness, is that it is only at worst going to last for a few weeks, and that unless you are very unlucky it will quickly pass off during the day. Most important of all is to remember the principles of good nutrition: getting enough to eat, and getting the right mixture of foods – fruit and vegetables, some meat, eggs or fish, milk or cheese now and then, topped up with bread or cake. Even though you may feel terrible in the morning, you should eat really good meals later on in the day.

SWOLLEN ANKLES

This condition, usually due to a slight increase in blood pressure, occurs in about a quarter of all women who are having their first baby, and in about 10 per cent of women having their second or subsequent babies. Usually it is not a serious problem. So long as you feel well, there is no need for you to change your eating habits nor to drink less than usual, provided the swelling goes down in a day or two. This generally happens if, as soon as you notice the situation, you take proper measures to deal with it: cutting down on the salt in your food, making sure that you get plenty of sleep at night, and taking a couple of hours rest with your feet up during the afternoon. If the swelling does not soon go down and particularly if your hands, face or abdomen swell as well, you should consult a doctor at once. Again, as with morning sickness, the scientific reason for the condition is not fully understood.

ADDING WEIGHT – OR NOT

A great many women nowadays fuss about their weight, and, whenever anyone talks about diet, jump to the conclusion that what is meant is a slimming diet. So I want to emphasise that whether you are pregnant or not, you need to consider not only whether you are as thin (or should I say 'slim') as you wish to be but also whether you are as fat (or ought I to say 'plump') as you ought to be.

When an overweight woman is pregnant, her chances of suffering from swollen ankles, and thus having to take particular care of herself, are slightly greater than if her weight were normal. For this and for all the other reasons which equally influence non-pregnant women, it is sensible not to be overweight before deciding to become pregnant. But if you are still overweight at the end of the first three months of pregnancy, not only ought you *not* to take drastic steps to lose weight but you must also resign yourself to putting on more weight.

By the time half your pregnancy is up (that is, after about twenty weeks), it is normal and healthy for you to have put on about 8 lb. Thereafter, you ought to be eating and drinking enough to put on a pound or so each week. If you are 'eating for two' sensibly, therefore, you can expect to weigh 2 stone (28 lb) more after nine months of pregnancy than you did before.

Individual women differ. Some put on more weight than this during pregnancy and come to no harm, and others put on less. Minor differences are nothing to fuss about. If, however, you are *not* gaining weight, or are gaining less than, say, half a pound a week during the last few months of your pregnancy, then either you are ill or you are not getting enough to eat. On the other hand, if you are putting on maybe 2 lb a week or so, it may not be a simple case of overeating. High blood pressure may be involved as well.

ANAEMIA

I have already explained why it is important for a pregnant woman to eat more iron than usual. But regardless of whether they obtain enough iron or not, two or three pregnant women in every hundred develop a kind of anaemia which is due to a shortage not of iron but of a vitamin ('folic acid') which is naturally present in green vegetables and a number of other foods (and this underlines all that I have said about the importance of eating a mixture of different foods). Most welfare centres and the doctors who plan their programmes give the vitamin to their expectant mothers in tablet form.

More Salt or Less?

Where the seasoning of food with salt is concerned, there are wide differences in taste. Some people – and some pregnant women – like much more salt in their food than others do. But there is usually no need to fuss. Indeed, you may even find it useful actually to increase the amount of salt you eat if you are one of those who suffer periodically from cramp. This usually affects a calf muscle and can be exceedingly painful, and it is particularly troublesome when it occurs in the middle of the night. Cramp is sometimes – but not always – caused by a lack of sufficient salt in the diet to counterbalance the amount of salt lost in sweat. It may afflict pregnant and non-pregnant women alike. If it is found that attacks are prevented by slightly increasing the amount of salt used in cooking or taken as a condiment, such an increase is obviously sensible. All the same, eating *much too much salt* can be dangerous during pregnancy; and, in particular, this should be avoided if you notice that your ankles are swollen.

A Note about Drinks

Most of this chapter concerns what you ought to eat when you are pregnant. But what you should drink is also worth considering. Milk is valuable, particularly during the second half of pregnancy. But apart from drinks like milk and orange juice which contribute to the value of your diet as a whole, it is a useful practice to drink a glass of water first thing in the morning, at meals and possibly also in the evening.

Although it is not necessary for you to give up drinking alcohol altogether when you are pregnant, you should take it only in *very* moderate quantities. Although alcohol has not been clearly proved to harm the unborn child there is a possibility that it may do so, particularly if taken to excess. Since it is important for you not to fuss, a glass of what you fancy now and then is unlikely to do you or the baby any harm. A full-blown party or a night out 'with the boys' may cause non-pregnant party-goers little more than a transient headache the following morning. You should remember, however, that your baby shares your bloodstream and that when what is carried round in it on 'the morning after' causes you to feel under the weather, the baby will suffer too. But he may suffer permanently. So it is wise to exercise moderation in this, as in so many other activities.

Whims and Humours

Not long ago, many women used to expect that when they were going to have a baby they would find themselves longing for some strange and unusual food, and that they would find themselves swept by fits of temper. *Because* they expected to hunger for shrimps or sheep's heart and to fly into a tantrum at the drop of a saucer – they often *did*. Over the last forty years or so, however, women have become more closely integrated into the general busyness of the community, and nowadays far fewer women experience these whims. Some women, however, do undoubtedly develop some kind of craving when they are pregnant. Probably the most common is a general longing for food: such a woman finds herself with an enormous appetite. Obviously, if you give way to this kind of capricious hankering for food you will become fat. So it is sensible to grit your teeth and make up your mind to fight this particular whim.

If you have a craving for some fairly ordinary food, even if it is something you do not normally eat, there is no reason why you should not have it provided you do not eat so much of it as to upset the balance of your diet as a whole. Try, however, to avoid heartburn and indigestion, which can be particularly troublesome towards the end of pregnancy; you will probably quickly come to recognise the kinds of food which disagree with you.

By no means all pregnant women develop peculiar whims about food and it is usually impossible to discover any scientific reason why a woman hankers after any particular item. It would be harsh to suggest that some of these whims arise from nervousness, idleness (dare I say it?) or a hidden desire to attract attention, and certainly this is by no means always true. Some bizarre cravings are very strong.

The Contented Mind and Body

Pregnancy is a peculiarly important time in a woman's life, and a time of joy and pride to the family to which she belongs. Always, she feels a sense of wonder at the new life she is going to bring into the world out of the unknowable nothingness of the unborn. And the responsibility for the future rests on her husband. The children, too, know that something important and unusual is happening, and sense that they will have to move over and make room for a stranger.

No wonder an expectant mother sometimes worries about her health and diet. No wonder she may develop fanciful fads and whims. Yet it is not difficult for her to organise her diet properly. Even though she does have special needs, particularly later in pregnancy, in the main all she requires is a good mixed diet, with some extra milk and perhaps some mineral and vitamin tablets. But in addition it is essential for her to feel herself to be part of her family. If the family can so arrange affairs that they all sit down together for meals there is a better chance that she will actually eat that good mixed diet. But every bit as important is the support that her united family provides. Joining in their activities will leave her less time to worry or to fancy herself unwell, their healthy concern will quell her apprehensions, and should she be bothered by one or other of the disorders of pregnancy, their sympathy will help her to overcome them.

FOUR

Younger Eaters

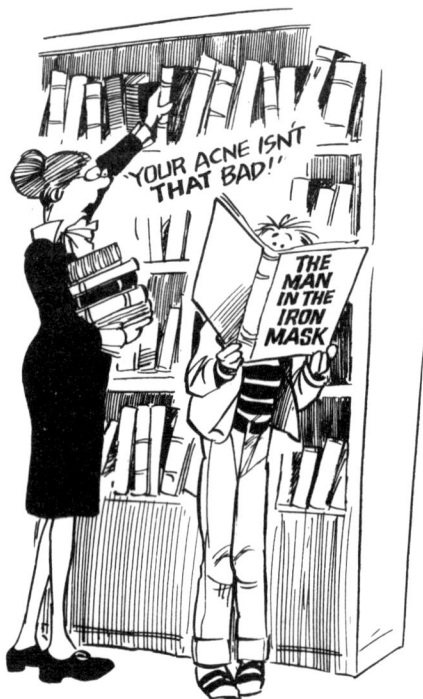

'. . . it is unfortunately true that boys suffer cruelly from acne round about the age of puberty.'

THERE ARE two kinds of teenager: young women and young men. For both, the period of adolescence possesses a number of important nutritional implications. Some of them are due to the physiological changes that take place during this particularly testing time of life. But perhaps still more significant are the social forces which exert important influences on young people.

Many of the primitive societies – where very little was known about nutrition, and what was known was sometimes not much more than magic – guarded their teenagers closely, looked after them well and fed them on food considered appropriate for their needs: these were, after all, the virgins who were the future mothers of the tribe, and the young warriors subjecting themselves to ordeals regarded as an honour to undergo for the future strength and well-being of the group. It is paradoxical that today's clever, self-confident society, which we suppose to have advanced to a peak of civilised living never previously attained, seems far less conscious of the importance of its teenagers. No effort is made to keep them in the parental home; on the contrary, the parents are almost glad when the youngsters leave. They find a 'pad' wherever they can. They do not all know how to cook, nor do they always put aside enough money to buy adequate food. They may lead a disorderly life and keep irregular hours. Some experiment with drink or marijuana which reduces their appetite for food, leaves them with less money to buy it with and confuses them when they choose what food to buy. All too often, their special needs are overlooked altogether.

What Teenage Boys Need

What is so special for a teenage boy in the physical sense is puberty, a fairly abrupt change which you can expect to take place when a boy is about fifteen years old. If you have been marking off your son's height year by year on the bathroom door, the first sign you will have that puberty is imminent will be a sudden burst of growth. Whereas your son and heir has been growing steadily at a rate of an inch or so a year, all at once he will be found to be perhaps an inch and a half or two inches taller than he was on his last birthday. Then it all begins to happen. His voice breaks, his Adam's apple starts to stick out, and the next thing you will notice is that he really does need to shave (although the fashionable ideas of his group may require him to grow a fluffy beard instead).

The exact age of puberty may vary by several years – as any observant choirmaster knows. But bearing in mind these variations, there is no doubt that over a group as a whole, the age of puberty is influenced by the level of nutrition of the group: how much the schoolboy eats and how nourishing his meals are has a direct effect on the age at which he reaches puberty and becomes, in the fullest sense, a 'teenager'.

No one would want knowingly to underfeed a little boy, even though it is generally assumed that, after a difficult start in life, Oliver Twist enjoyed a prosperous adulthood. Just the same, there are certain facts which suggest that the last word in scientific enlightenment may not invariably be represented by the modern insistence that children should be crammed with as much of every vitamin, protein and mineral as they can conceivably use, and that they should never under any circumstances be subjected to hardship – and should certainly *never* be sent to bed without their suppers. All this may mean that the onset of puberty is brought forward. But is it good to reach puberty early?

For the teenager himself there are two possible advantages. He is likely to be somewhat bigger, not only sooner but probably throughout his life, than if he had had less to eat when young. And he will, of course, become sexually capable sooner – which can be either good or bad.

On the other hand, later puberty implies that the young fellow will get by on less food, which is an advantage should food be scarce. A more substantial advantage is suggested by evidence that an individual who has overcome hardship in his youth may actually live longer than one who has enjoyed soft living and luxury in his childhood.

ENOUGH FOOD AND EXERCISE

Somehow or other a boy needs to extract enough nourishment from his food to enable him to grow about eight inches taller and three stone heavier during the growth spurt that accompanies puberty. But in order to fit the diet to the teenager we need to know what kind of a teenager we are talking about.

Lively and vigorous. The active young fellow, always on the go and probably often in trouble, the boy who plays energetic games and does not merely stand about watching other people playing – this kind of teenager needs to eat a lot. He is best off nutritionally if he has a sensible mother who provides a large cooked breakfast; if a large cooked midday meal comes his way most days at least, if not every day; and if a large cooked evening meal is also usually available. If that is so, then meat, eggs, fish, potatoes and other vegetables, not to speak of bread and jam and cake, are all part of his dietary intake; and then there is enough nutritional ballast to cope with the snacks – the bottles of sweet soft drinks, the chocolate bars, the packets of crisps and all the miscellaneous and extravagant items of promiscuous eating which the voracious teenager, quite rightly – because his needs are large – will want to buy and eat. Parents who still look after teenagers of this sort at home should be particularly careful that they get good food from the ice-boxes they raid and find solid nourishment in the cake tins and biscuit boxes they dip into.

Languid and lethargic. Not all teenage boys are noisy, rowdy and active. Others are bowed down with the troubles of the world and with the sorrows of being spurned by girls (or worse still, yearning to be popular with them but lack nerve to try) and spend long hours lying on their beds brooding, or trying to write poetry, or listening interminably to records. These young men need to be tempted to eat, but not to eat too much. If there is ever a time for a mother to become fussy about vitamins and proteins, this is it. Otherwise such an adolescent may eat too much bread and jam, steamed pudding and cake out of sheer frustration and longing for comfort. Should this happen, the boy will become fat.

Or it can happen that an introspective adolescent will become so far weighed down by the problems and difficulties of his age that he may eat too little, and that what he does eat may not be what he needs. If he has his meals at home, he needs to be tempted to drink his breakfast orange juice and to eat a salad now and then, and not be allowed to get by on a hurried sandwich as he darts out to the disco. And no matter how annoying and undisciplined he may seem, however rude and ungrateful and – most irritating of all – *never* around when meals are on the table, it is a real nutritional duty of love for his mother to find some way to get him to eat freshly cooked potatoes and greens – *not* vegetables that have been kept hot for a couple of hours waiting for him to come in.

There are problems too for the indolent and perhaps disorganised teenager who lives alone in a bedsitter and looks after his own catering. One difficulty may be that he has no proper cooking facilities in his room. This is made worse if no cooked midday meal is available for him at school or college or at his place of work, or if the meals that are available are tired and unpalatable from having been stacked up on metal rings and kept hot for hours, or so inconvenient and expensive that he does not want or cannot afford to buy them.

I repeat: cooking is not *essential* for good nutrition. But the desirable diverse mixture of potatoes and greens, peas and carrots is difficult to provide if you have no proper stove, or if your cooking skill is restricted to fried eggs. There is, of course, no need for a teenager to suffer if he makes sure that once or twice a week he eats an apple, an orange, a tomato or – in the season – a pound of cherries. But he must make sure of two things: that he remembers to buy these items, and that he has enough money to do so. One of the great nutritional advantages of a household where cooking goes on all the time is that a sensible housekeeper (who may be the mother but can equally well be a properly organised youngster who knows what he is doing) can make use of whole cabbage and cauliflowers and seven-pound bags of potatoes and so forth; this means that she can serve interestingly varied meals more cheaply than can a solitary individual buying in fruit and sliced ham and even chocolate bars and crisps (an expensive method of eating) in single helpings.

Health for Girls

Girls, like boys, experience an abrupt spurt in growth as they pass through the age of puberty. The gains in weight and height are usually less than in boys and occur about two years sooner. This is the time when the girl who has bullied her little brother throughout their childhood is overtaken by him in height and weight. As with boys, although individual girls reach puberty at widely differing ages, well-fed girls reach puberty on average sooner than those receiving a less good diet.

Puberty for girls is, of course, indicated more precisely than in boys. It is marked by the onset of menstruation. We can look back across history to, say, 1870 when food was dear and wages scanty and when working girls were shut up in the dormitories of the factories of the worst period of the Industrial Revolution; there are statistics from Great Britain, other European countries and the swelling immigrant towns of the United States showing that the average age of menstruation was then over sixteen years (so far as an average can be struck from the available records). By 1900 welfare schemes were beginning to appear on the scene, and the average age of puberty had dropped to about fifteen. Thirty years later again, the figures were still falling. By now, however, the more rapidly improving conditions in the United States were beginning to have some effect, and their better-fed girls began to mature even earlier than those in Europe. The average by now – that is 1930 – was about fourteen years. By the time we come to the 1960s, when in the community at large food was more plentiful and it was recognised that girls, just like their brothers, deserved enough to eat, the average age of puberty was somewhere around thirteen.

After puberty, several things happen to the nutritional needs of a girl. The first is that, since her spurt of growth is over, the total amount of food she needs is reduced. And unless she is an enthusiastic sportswoman, it is further reduced because she is now no longer a tomboy schoolgirl but a young lady who has given up tearing around the streets. Moreover, since she is now likely to begin to worry more about her appearance, she may decide to eat less so as to keep slim.

Good Advice: Part One to the adolescent girl is that, while giving up steamed puddings, toffee bars and bottles of sweetened soft drinks (and going light on any boxes of chocolates she may be given by admiring boyfriends), she should nevertheless take care not to go to the other extreme and eat too little from the mistaken idea that all thin girls are breathtakingly beautiful.

Once her menstruation begins, she needs to obtain enough iron in her food to enable her to replace what she loses each month.

Good Advice: Part Two is therefore that even if she does not want to eat a large meal, it is sensible to go for corned beef or tongue or indeed any other meat, either from the hot meal at home or in the canteen, or from the insides of sandwiches. It is better nutritional sense for her to eat meat than to drink milk. Milk is indeed full of protein (and has a good deal of fat in it as well) and contains calcium, but for adolescents as well as for most adults its dietetic virtues are over-sold. The adolescent girl can get plenty of protein from her normal meals without having extra milk. She may well, however, be short of iron; but there is almost no iron in milk, while meat and the socially despised black pudding make very useful contributions.

Good Advice: Part Three (Part Four coming later!). Like everyone else, a teenage girl should vary what goes into her meals, if not from day to day, then at least as the weeks go by. It is quite satisfactory to eat bread every day but now and then meat and eggs must play a part, and milk and cheese too. The prejudice about potatoes only does harm: having potatoes every day is fine if you like them. And potatoes no more 'make you fat' than do bread and butter, baked beans or rice pudding; whether you get fat or not depends on the amount you eat in relation to the amount you need. Finally, there should always be vegetables and fruit in the diet – greens or tomatoes, lettuce or carrots, apples, cherries, strawberries or plums, whatever is in season. Bad nutrition is the lazy life of someone who subsists on, say, hot dogs day after day without a change.

Those Damned Spots

Teenagers, and particularly boys, are often sensitive about their complexions. Some of them have good cause to be sensitive because it is unfortunately true that boys suffer cruelly from acne round about the age of puberty. But providing that you have been eating a mixture of food items in your meals, there is nothing you can do about your bad complexion by eating oranges, oily sardines, platefuls of carrots or handfuls of vitamin tablets. In other words, food and nutrition play little or no part in deciding whether you will be spotty or not.

Looking Your Best

A good and healthy diet is something that all sensible teenagers want to eat. At the same time, there are other things to which they give higher priority. The first of these is the apparently urgent business of getting away from their parents' home. This may be bad for their nutrition, particularly if their mothers, careful housewives and good cooks though they may be, have not passed on their skills to their sons and daughters.

Secondly, teenagers are often for the first time earning money. Although like everyone else they would like to earn more, they believe that their earnings are, all things considered, quite enough to enable them to live tolerably well. After all, they have usually no one to spend their money on except themselves.

Thirdly, high up on their scale of priorities, very often higher even than 'having a good time' and certainly a long way above eating sensibly, comes their desire to look nice. It does not matter whether they are young men or young women; the boys and girls are in this together, each wanting to please the other. The trouble is that nowadays it is increasingly expensive to keep up with the fashion because fashions change very quickly and also because there are several fashions to keep up with. Years ago, when miniskirts first came in, all the girls rushed to buy them; but at least they remained *de rigueur* for a reasonable length of time before some other fashion which 'everyone' had to wear arrived to take their place. Today things are different. One week a magazine will tell you that frizzy hair, ponchos and beads are in fashion, together with tight jeans, cowboy shirts and platform shoes; in the next issue you are urged to go out and buy knee-length boots and maxiskirts. Almost every week there comes an urgent demand to spend money in order to keep up with the changing demands of 'looking nice'.

If the weekly money drains away on clothes, however, there may not be enough left to buy proper food. If you are studying how to be a well-fed teenager, it is far more important for you to discover how to put by the amount of money it takes to buy enough food than to learn by heart how much vitamin B_{12} there is in calves' liver. Good wages are a delusion if they are spent on the wrong things. There is nothing wrong with wanting to 'look good'. Just the same, if you spend so much money on fashionable clothes and 'with-it' gear that you have too little for food, it will not be long before you cease to look your best.

Good Advice: Part Four. Spend enough money on food at least to make sure that you are not hungry. Even this is not sufficient to keep you fit and well for long unless you put by enough for at least one splendid meal a week (one a day is better but one a week may be easier, because good cooking does take time). This should comprise a meat dish, potatoes, greens, pudding, cheese, maybe fruit as well – the lot! Such a meal will be money well – and enjoyably – spent.

Good Appetites

Good nutrition depends on good appetite. Milk and meat and cheese, no matter how full of animal protein, orange juice no matter how packed with vitamin C and liver no matter how rich in vitamin A – none of these does you any good if you don't have the appetite to eat them. Most teenagers have good appetites. Most have an appetite that tells them to eat when they are hungry, to go on eating until they have had enough (not merely enough for pleasure but enough to satisfy their nutritional needs) and then stop. A few teenagers – fewer than many teenage girls imagine – have an appetite that does not tell them to stop eating until after they have eaten a little more than they really need. These are the young people with a tendency to become fat.

GIRLS WHO DON'T EAT

Sometimes a girl quite suddenly loses her appetite, stops eating and becomes really ill. Although this doesn't happen very often, it is probably more common than any adverse effects arising from not drinking orange juice or not eating greens, and certainly more often met with than any shortage of protein, matters on which nutritionists have in the past had much more to say.

What usually happens is this. A girl may have been fussing about her food. Perhaps she has got it into her head that a certain boy does not fancy her because she is too fat, even though she is really rather thin. Or perhaps her friends have been boasting about their success with men while she knows that she is herself too shy to do the sorts of things they do (or at least *say* they do). Or she may have quarrelled with her boyfriend, possibly because his idea of making love goes beyond what she is prepared to agree to. Or she may be on bad terms with her mother. The exact cause of her unhappiness may seem quite trivial and unimportant, but just the same, she loses any desire to eat. Very often she finds bread and butter, toast and cake actively disgusting and, if she eats anything at all, it will be meat and vegetables. And she picks even at these, and takes longer and longer between mouthfuls. All this can lead to serious malnutrition; girls affected in this way can actually starve themselves to death. The sort of girls who suffer are not fools. Indeed, they may be those who are particularly reliable and conscientious.

Even though this loss of appetite is rare, it is useful for you to know that it can happen, whether or not you are yourself a teenager. Firstly, if it is happening to you and you have the wit to realise it, you may have enough strength of character to pull yourself out of it by your own efforts, and gradually to get back your appetite by eating. The second reason is that you may see it happening to someone else, and may be able at least to help to save her.

The best treatment – almost the only treatment – is love and persistence. If you feel real affection for a girl (as distinct from the mushy self-indulgence dressed up in pop songs) and you see her going through this sort of nutritional crisis, you can certainly help her by acting as a devoted friend. In extreme cases such girls can be taken into hospital but even then the outcome is uncertain. A patient boyfriend, a loyal girl friend, a wise mother – any of these must be prepared to put up with what can seem an infuriating and self-destructive resistance to eating, but may in the end, slowly and gradually, see the girl's appetite return.

All this illustrates in an extreme way the relationship between your body's working as a biochemical machine and at the same time as part of an individual. Your appetite is controlled by a special organ, the hypothalamus, situated underneath your brain. It in its turn is triggered off by the concentration of sugar in your blood and a number of other factors. But at the same time this whole system is affected by what is happening to you at the time. Some people may eat too much when they are bored or miserable. Others eat too little. And the way in which young people feel, whether they are happy or unhappy, is very much influenced by those around them; their nutrition is thus directly related to the kind of 'gang' they belong to and by the way this 'gang' behaves.

Discos, Drink and Pot

Dancing and music are fun; but they do need to be fitted into a sensible daily life. A teenager may, perhaps, get up too late in the morning to have more than a cup of tea for breakfast, and may then have just a hot dog and a bottle of Coke for lunch; if he misses his main evening meal because of the urge to rush out to the disco – then even if there has been enough to eat, the proper mixture cannot be made up.

The same kind of thing applies to drink or pot. Too much drink may make the drinker fat. The most direct effect (and it is a negative one) of drinking or smoking 'joints' is, however, that long, long sessions of aimless talking take the place of mealtimes which, if properly organised, can be just as agreeable a forum for the exchange of views, and nourishing as well.

Most important of all, when money has been spent on communal pleasures like these it is no longer available for food.

On Not Being a Stranger

Most populous industrial countries afford sanctuary to minority groups. For instance, for several generations people have come to Great Britain from the Caribbean, from India, Sri Lanka and China, and from different parts of Africa. Many of their descendants now live and speak – and eat – just like the people whose families have always lived in Great Britain. The nutritional advice in this book is as apt for these people as for everyone else. But some of those whose families once came from overseas want to keep to their old ways of eating (or their parents do, so that whether they want to or not the teenagers must do so as well). For these there may be particular hazards.

BREAD

Ordinary British bread is not as ordinary as it looks. For thirty years or more the British public-health authorities have ruled that bakers must add two of the B-vitamins, some iron and some calcium to their white bread. Some families who hailed originally from overseas still eat chapatis or cassava instead of bread. But if they stick rigidly to what the old folks ate, they may get into trouble in the cold, cloudy British climate where things are very different from where chapatis and cassava are traditionally eaten, and where money is more important and there may not be enough of it to go round. It is prudent for them to mix a little Marmite (containing B-vitamins) in the curry, to add powdered milk to top up their calcium as well, and to eat meat each week – whether it is a proper joint or mince, hamburger, sausage, liver or kidney does not matter – to make sure that they have enough iron. This may be difficult but it is worth doing just the same.

BUTTER AND MARGARINE

British families that eat butter eat a great deal of it because of the British custom of spreading it on bread. In fact, big families, and families without much money, probably eat more butter than their more prosperous neighbours do, because they tend to eat fewer cooked meals and more sandwiches (in which the bread is buttered) and bread and butter. The British also eat margarine, which is usually cheaper than butter, and which, on the insistence of the public-health authorities, contains vitamin A and vitamin D. British teenagers obtain much of their needs of these vitamins from butter and margarine, particularly if they do not trouble to cook themselves each week at least one proper meal.

Teenagers who choose to eat as their grandparents did, rather than as their mates do, can get their vitamin A by eating plenty of greens and carrots. To obtain vitamin D, these young people could perhaps regularly eat herrings (which may be expensive or difficult to find), or they could buy cod-liver oil or vitamin D tablets from a chemist (but these can be expensive too and this is not really a sensible way to put one's diet right). But there is another way to get vitamin D besides eating it. This is to get out into the sunshine as much as possible, because skin can itself make vitamin D if sunlight is allowed to fall upon it. This has many advantages: in the summer, sunbathing is fun, and even in winter outdoor sports in the sun and fresh air are healthy and encourage a good appetite. But teenagers whose ancestors came from sunny countries in Asia or Africa – where they could make nearly all the vitamin D they needed for themselves – must understand that Great Britain is by and large a grey, chilly country where perpetual sunshine is only a travel agent's dream, and that the traditional British diet has been modified to deal with this climate, for example, by vitamin D being added to the margarine. If people choose to eat a non-British diet while living in Britain, therefore, they should remember that such a diet was developed to fit very different circumstances.

Cheaper Eaters

'I can have nothing but praise for a "ploughman's lunch"...'

THE SINGLE DEFICIENCY which, above all, causes malnutrition is a deficiency of *money*, with a deficiency of knowledge running it a close second.

Perhaps we should first define what we mean by poverty. Whenever there is an industrial dispute, the negotiators argue that the workers cannot exist any longer on whatever it is they are being paid, whether it is three, four or five thousand pounds a year. This implies that in an industrial country these sums, in the view of responsible men and women, represent poverty. But in other parts of the world, similar incomes would represent wealth. Indeed, there are many people living in the developed countries of the west who find such incomes sufficiently ample for them to send substantial sums to their relatives in far poorer communities across the seas. Poverty, therefore, is compounded of two parts: the first is measured by what the income will buy, while the second depends on the expectations of the individual whose income it is. Hence we come to the definition of poverty as *having an income insufficient to enable its possessors to purchase the things which they expect to enjoy as members of the community to which they consider they belong*.

This view of poverty influences each one of us, and it has a very direct effect on our state of nutrition. If you were impoverished by a prolonged spell of unemployment, you would have to be hard pressed indeed before you gave up your accustomed luxuries, whether they are your mid-morning cups of coffee or your evening visits to the pub. The distressed gentlewoman will be distressed indeed rather than fail to provide her cat with a diet which may even cost more than her own. We have to accept that an individual – or of course, his family – may suffer from malnutrition due to poverty even though his income would represent riches to Sri Lankan peasants or squatters in

Calcutta. This being so, it is worth considering how people can use nutritional knowledge to eat cheaply and thus stave off this most potent of all deficiency factors: a deficiency of money.

What Are You Paying For?

Fashion, custom, habit, history and downright snobbery – far more than nutritional value – are all involved in the cost of most of the foods eaten by the inhabitants of wealthy societies. (When the chips are down and food of any sort is *really* scarce, staple foods upon which people depend for their very lives begin to be recognised as being beyond price. A famine is a great way to clarify popular views about economics.) Nor is it altogether easy to argue whether or not some high-priced foodstuffs are worth their cost on account of the deliciousness of their taste. Part of the pleasure they give may arise because they are what is sometimes called 'up market', and the satisfaction they provide – like that from a diamond ring – may come from demonstrating that one can afford to buy them. Assuming that you are prepared to forgo this kind of satisfaction, let us consider a few items that are poor value in terms of nutrition for the money that is spent on them – spent, in fact, for quite different reasons.

CAVIAR

If you are poor, don't bother to buy caviar. And however rich you are, don't buy it if you suffer from gout; caviar, like other fish roes, contains substances which gouty people do well to avoid. It is one of the sociological curiosities of the age that anyone in his senses should be prepared to pay the price asked for caviar. No other food costs anything like as much as this, which when all's said and done is nothing more than rather salty fish paste. Indeed, during the First World War some of the soldiers fighting in Turkey who were issued with caviar as part of their rations objected strongly to what we are told they described as 'blankety-blank fish jam'!

OYSTERS

Oysters are agreeable minor articles of diet which admirably accompany brown bread and butter and stout to form a simple meal that, if complemented with a good squeeze of lemon, provides virtually all the necessary vitamins. Only a century ago, before oysters became fashionable and when, like whelks and cockles today, they were good value for money, poor people for whom meat was an expensive luxury showed good nutritional judgement in eating them in quantity. Today, however, oysters – like seats at the opera – are ridiculously dear, and only people who are passionately devoted to their taste and smell and to the shivery feeling they give as they slide down the gullet would think of buying them. On nutritional grounds, oysters haven't a leg to stand on (if I may use the expression). You could, in fact, just as well eat the brown bread in the form of a meat-paste sandwich.

SMOKED SALMON

Although no woman with a family to feed and not much money would dream of buying it, it is interesting to consider how smoked salmon attained its grotesque cost and what happened when it did so.

Salmon was once a commonplace food in Scotland. Farm servants used to insist when they were engaged for a year's work that, if food was provided as part of their wages – as the custom was in those days – they should *not* be given salmon more than twice a week. Because the salmon is a big fish and because a lot of them may be caught all at once in favourable weather, the smoking process was used to try to preserve at least some of the fish for as long as possible.

When other more convenient methods of preserving fish, such as canning, became available, smoking became less common. Nowadays, for those who want nutritional value there is canned salmon (or canned tuna or pilchards) while for those who are prepared to pay dearly to enjoy the traditional taste of salmon smoked, or for those who are snobbish enough to believe that it improves their social image to be seen eating it at exorbitant cost, smoked salmon is still available, ready-cut into paper-thin slices. As with oysters, what was once an everyday food eaten by ordinary people was given up, it would seem without a struggle, when its price became too high.

STEAK

At different times, different parts of the ox have been held at varying levels of esteem. Parson Woodforde, who lived in the late 18th century, was very partial to ribs although he ate with relish different parts of all sorts of animals indiscriminately: saddle of mutton, pig's head, hares (of which he was particularly fond) and game birds of all kinds. In our own time, it would seem that as one moves backwards from the ox's nose to its tail, the meat is held to be more and more attractive; the esteem in which rump steak is held is very high and its price is correspondingly high too. It is true that steak can be quickly and easily cooked, that it is free from bone and excessive fat, has an agreeable flavour and consistency when it is cooked and is, furthermore, convenient to eat. Yet the nutritional value of steak is no higher than that of any other kind of meat that contains roughly the same amount of fat. It is, therefore, unreasonable for people to spend money on steak if their finances are limited and they are finding difficulty in affording enough food for themselves and their families. Most sensible people have in fact grasped this truth, not by studying textbooks on nutritional science or by taking up the latest fad about 'whole foods' or 'biological farming' (whatever these terms are supposed to mean) but by using common sense. Once again, consumers have to decide to what extent they are prepared to forgo the undoubted aesthetic pleasure of eating juicy steak in order to obtain an equivalent amount of nourishment more cheaply. The pleasure can, after all, be obtained in alternative ways. A good cook can do a lot of appetising things with cheaper cuts, such as skirt or shin of beef. And something very roughly approximating to steak can be constructed out of mince – what is usually called a hamburger. So far as nutrition is concerned, *any* sort of meat combined with cereals and vegetables provides the body with its needs. Meat and potato pie and steak and kidney pudding are excellent examples of such mixtures, and so are all the various kinds of stews and goulashes.

DOVER SOLE

Dover sole or, for that matter, turbot or red mullet or any of the other exotic fishes found on the menus of the posh restaurants, may be good value as providers of aesthetic satisfaction and entertainment, but nutritionally they are poor value for money and not in the running when compared with coley or whiting. And since much of the price of fresh fish arises from the need to transport it to market as quickly as possible and to keep it cool while doing so, modern technology contributes to bringing down the cost of fish in making available canned pilchards and canned mackerel, frozen fish fingers and the like.

All the foregoing shows is that we eat what we eat because we are used to a particular kind of diet, and because we enjoy the kinds of food we are used to. But if the price of a certain food goes up, we are compelled to change what we eat, and provided that we use our knowledge and common sense, such change can be made without necessarily damaging the nutritional value of our diet.

Cut-price Nutrition: Stage 1

Unless you are very unlucky, you are unlikely to become really poor all at once. More usually, one finds oneself encountering more and more difficulty in making ends meet. Alternatively, the amount of money available for housekeeping diminishes when other costs – fares, rates, mortgage payments or unlucky business demands – take precedence. Though times are hard, the situation has not yet become desperate. Under these circumstances it is comparatively easy to save money on food with no loss of nutritional value. Nor is it necessary to make a radical change in the kinds of foods that go into the daily menu. That only comes when the situation makes it necessary to move on to Stage 2.

CHEAPENING BREAKFAST

Cornflakes and milk are popular for breakfast. But there is a degree of extravagance in buying maize which, in Great Britain at least, has to be imported, and which is eaten only after it has been processed by sophisticated machinery in a cornflakes factory and packed in moisture-proof wrapping in a carton. Much the same nutritional value could be derived from bread and milk or from porridge made from home-grown oats, as used to be eaten before cornflakes were heard of.

Bacon and egg, though agreeable, can no longer be considered cheap. The nutritional value of the diet, however, can be tolerably well maintained without a cooked breakfast, as fifty million Frenchmen (not to mention almost all the rest of the population of the European Economic Community) have always been aware. This does not mean that people should go without breakfast altogether: something to eat first thing is nutritionally useful. But just as a Frenchman eats his *croissant* with his breakfast coffee, an Englishman could do as well to eat his buttered toast and marmalade.

Most people now recognise that butter is broadly-speaking the nutritional equivalent of margarine, and if money is scarce and margarine is less expensive than butter – as it usually is – they buy margarine to spread on their breakfast toast. If money should become very scarce indeed, a further saving could be made by using the dripping remaining in the frying pan or the roasting tin after cooking, to spread on the bread. Now, however, the importance of nutritional knowledge becomes apparent. Both butter and margarine, besides making dry bread taste nicer, contribute vitamin A to the diet; dripping does not. This is unimportant provided that you get the vitamin from somewhere else, such as carrots. Luckily carrots, whether raw or cooked, are both cheap and popular with children.

CHEAPENING THE MIDDAY MEAL

Any sensible person knows that the simplest way to save money on the midday meal is to turn it into a packed lunch. When money is short, the 'best buy' on nutritional terms is one of the cereal crops that has kept us all going for thousands of years. Rice serves this function in the east; for ourselves it is wheat, either as bread or as flour.

Nowadays, sandwiches are the way in which we demonstrate our increasing dependence on wheat and bread. Whether filled with meat or cheese, peanut butter or jam, pilchards or paste, sandwiches benefit from being supplemented by an orange or an apple, a few slices of tomato or, at the very least, a gherkin. The so-called 'ploughman's lunch' also illustrates how people seek to eat cheaply by increasing their dependence on bread. I can have nothing but praise for a 'ploughman's lunch', made up of a hunk of thickly buttered bread, a chunk of cheese and a tomato or spring onion – and it is growing in popularity just at the very time when ploughmen are becoming conspicuously rare.

CHEAPENING THE EVENING MEAL

Obviously, the first step is to do without high-priced luxury foods, even though this may be hard for those who thrill to the taste of smoked salmon and oysters and the smell of sizzling steak, regardless of the equal nutritional value of pilchards and mince. The next step is to combine what little meat and fish you can afford – and *all* kinds of meat and fish are relatively expensive – by using them as minority ingredients in dishes like shepherd's pie or Irish stew, or (for fish) in fish pie, fish cakes or kedgeree, which is a mixture of fish, eggs and rice. The third step is to look back in history to less affluent and less luxurious times. Take, for instance, the often under-rated baked bean. When baked beans first emerged as a popular mass-produced article they still bore some similarity to the rough food of the poor cow-hands who first invented them. Travelling with their herds, these men carried with them a sack of dry beans and a hunk of salt pork. When they camped for the night, they heated up some of the beans that they had soaked, and added a piece of the salt pork to the pan over the camp fire. This diet, though monotonous, was as nourishing as they could achieve with cheap, portable foods that would keep well. The first cans of baked beans still included the traditional lump of fat pork in every can, and this greatly improved the nutritional value of the dish: the vegetable protein of the beans enhanced the animal protein of the pork. Now that the pork has vanished from our canned beans, it is useful to top the family's beans on toast with a rasher of bacon or a poached egg instead. Tomato sauce or, better still, tomato itself or cabbage or, indeed, potato would turn the mixture into a really first-class nutritional combination.

Texturised vegetable protein (TVP) is an attempt by the food technologists to raise the low esteem in which beans are held, and to improve their flavour and consistency until the product made from them can claim to be the equal of steak itself in its aesthetic qualities – taste, appearance and the way it feels when chewed. TVP, though primarily made out of beans, is nutritionally quite similar to meat, especially in the form of some of the newer 'knitted steak' products in which food scientists have co-operated with textile engineers to manufacture a structure in which bean fibres are bound together with a quantity of egg which, though small, is sufficient to complement the quality of the vegetable protein.

Years ago, puddings used to be eaten as an adjunct to meat, much as we still eat dumplings. Yorkshire pudding is almost the last example of pudding still being eaten in this way, although in toad-in-the-hole, another traditional dish, meat and pudding are mixed up together. A simple economy would be to eat more and more Yorkshire pudding – containing egg and milk as well as flour – and less and less roast beef. Nutrition would not suffer even if the contentment of the meat-lovers did; but then self-denial, whether compulsory or not, involves some degree of sacrifice.

Another approach to cheapening the main meal of the day is to take advantage of the simple and inexpensive dishes which already poor communities overseas have worked out for themselves. There is good sense, and good nutrition too, in a Briton who is short of money eating spaghetti and ravioli, macaroni and noodles, all of which have for years been the staple dishes of economical Italian countryfolk. These dishes are, of course, variations on the theme of supplementing cereals (wheat flour made into spaghetti, macaroni, noodles and the casing of the ravioli) by tasty sauces containing a modest amount of meat or cheese.

The same principle is illustrated by the recent growth in popularity of Indian restaurants and Chinese 'take-aways'. Indian dishes, other than those that are purely vegetarian, usually consist mainly of rice together with smaller amounts of meat, chicken or fish, while most Chinese meals are based on cereals and vegetables supplemented with eggs, fish and pork. An important lesson for western consumers is that cutting down on expensive meat need not damage the aesthetic interest of food, provided cooks use as much care in the preparation and flavouring of the cheaper ingredients as they do with steak and sole.

INDULGENCES

A lot of money is spent on things that are eaten or drunk between meals. Some of these, such as chewing gum, barely rank as foods at all; and money that in nutritional terms is badly spent is not merely wasted but, if poverty is really severe, can actually be damaging to nutrition.

Chocolate bars of various sorts are extensively advertised as providing energy, as 'bridging the energy-gap', or as keeping working men going (or elegant typists – it all depends on the advertisement). Of course, chocolate bars *do* provide energy-value; but so does buttered toast or bread and dripping, which are very much cheaper.

Tea and coffee provide no nutritional value at all apart from what is derived from the milk and sugar taken with them. So when you decide whether or not to pay the quite substantial costs of such beverages, you must estimate how important it is for you to enjoy their stimulating effects. People, if they put their minds to it, *can* give up smoking. Equally, they *can* give up cups of coffee or tea should they decide that the money thus saved could be spent to better advantage. Although this advice may read like nothing more than hard common sense, it is tough advice nevertheless. When the price of coffee began to soar sky-high a few years ago, people found that they could accustom themselves to drinking less of it, or to diluting it with chicory, or to using roasted acorns as a substitute – but they complained bitterly about having to do so. Common sense and strict adherence to nutritional principles can demand real strength of character.

Cut-price Nutrition: Stage 2

For people who are really very hard-up, there is considerable scope for putting together a very cheap but nutritionally adequate diet, if they are prepared to abandon many of their likes and dislikes, their prejudices and their ingrained ideas about the meals they have always regarded as both adequate and necessary.

BREAD AND WATER

The first dietetic essential to life is water. Next, bread, as a provider of the body's fuel, ranks high, at least in the west. But a diet of bread and water alone is nutritionally inadequate if adhered to for long.

Black bread and cabbage is a cheap, plain and very boring diet that was the traditional mainstay of people sent to Siberia. It is not particularly agreeable, but it is undoubtedly cheap. It is clearly an elaboration on bread and water. The cabbage provides vitamin C which is lacking in the bread and its leaf protein usefully complements the wheat protein. The weakness of such a diet is its lack of variety. Although it provides most of the nutrients required for immediate use, there are certain deficiencies that in time would cause trouble. However urgent it might be to reduce food costs to the minimum, it would be good sense to save up enough to buy a little butter now and then to spread on the bread and some sort of meat or an egg to improve the cabbage soup. If things were tough but not absolutely desperate, a diet as stringent as this could be used for an occasional week interspersed between weeks of more conventional meals.

Although the cheapest diet you could buy might be based on a sack of wheat bought from a farmer together with a bag of cabbages, this would present you with problems. Wheat is undoubtedly excellent nutritional value for money, and it keeps well. But it is difficult to convert it into an eatable condition in a domestic kitchen.

To start with, it is not easy to grind it up in, say, a coffee grinder, and domestic hand mills are quite expensive, as well as time-consuming to operate. This is why the miller, whether he operates a village water mill or a gigantic modern industrial plant, performs a valuable social service. Nevertheless, if you are proposing to try *cheap eating* and are prepared to bake your own bread, a moderately sized purchase of 'high-extraction' flour (i.e., wholemeal or wheatmeal) could be a good investment, as long as you don't pay a fancy 'health food' price for it.

PORRIDGE AND MILK

In the hard days of long ago, oatmeal and milk constituted the staple diet of crofters – that is, people living on small impoverished farms in Scotland. Oatmeal and oat flakes can still be bought cheaply from some millers and agricultural merchants, and can be converted into porridge without bringing the breakfast-food manufacturers or the cardboard-carton makers into the transaction. Porridge with milk, supplemented with vegetables, will provide most of the necessary nutrients. In Scottish terms, the vegetables might well be mashed neeps (turnips) or perhaps kale, reinforced now and then by at least a token portion of meat. Scottish butchers still follow the good nutritional tradition of the country by mincing up scraps of meat which less enlightened nations might call offal, and mixing them with onions and oatmeal to make haggis. (Outside Scotland the cheap eater must prepare the mixture for himself.) The combination of haggis and neeps makes an excellent and nutritious low-cost diet.

Poverty is not agreeable for those who enjoy the pleasures of the table, and who find a daily diet restricted to porridge, haggis and turnips tedious in the extreme. Nevertheless, the option is open. Most of us shrink from such a monotonous regime; and this underlines the importance of pleasure in the practice of dietetics.

POTATOES AND MILK

Just as Highland crofters once thrived largely on oatmeal and milk, so also a century ago and more the hard-pressed countryfolk of Ireland found that they could live and raise their families on a diet composed mainly of potatoes and milk. This mixture, though dangerously restricted, is virtually complete nutritionally, particularly if from time to time it is reinforced with a scrap of meat, a piece of fish or an egg. One drawback is that an active man needs to eat six to nine *pounds* of potatoes a day to obtain the energy-value he needs for his day's labour. This considerable weight is required because the moisture content of potatoes is so high – much higher than that of oatmeal or of bread.

BEANS

Dried beans or dried peas are good nutritional value for money, much more so than the canned variety. Either on their own, perhaps cooked to a mush like pease pudding, or mixed with cereals and vegetables, they are sustaining without costing very much, especially if they can be bought in bulk. Soya beans, which came originally from China but which are now grown on a large scale in the United States and elsewhere, are particularly useful, partly because, unlike other beans, they contain some fat and partly because their taste is comparatively mild and unbeany. Unfortunately, all beans encourage flatulence, which can be tiresome if you are eating them every day.

'Cheap Eats'

One of the most remarkable developments of our techno-logical age is the trend for people across the world to eat the same foods and the same products of food technology: not only people on world cruises who eat cornflakes, sliced bread and ice cream right round the globe, but also the ordinary citizens of New York, London, Bombay and

Tokyo. Gradually, industrially processed foods have become more and more widely adopted – as have wrist-watches and ballpoint pens. The implication is that many people – perhaps most people – *like* eating the conventional foods of the west, provided they have the money to buy them. But this liking is not universal – even in the west.

There are those who believe that a simple diet is best and who enjoy its simplicity quite apart from its cheapness. Some of these are people who feel that life should not be spent in pursuit of money, while others want to devote what money they have to other things. Often they use culinary skills to make simple foods more tasty and less tedious: there are delicious ways of cooking whole brown rice, either alone or with beans, of making rice balls, of simmering whole wheat grains with raisins to make frumenty, or of cooking it with peas and beans, of making a mixture of roasted wheat or rye grains with vegetables. You can find books concerned with this kind of cooking in 'whole food' shops.

These people have gone the whole hog, showing that it *is* possible to use wheat without calling in the miller to mill it, and that they can eat well without subjecting their food to modern technological processes, while actually enjoying plain simple meals that are quite unlike the sort of meals we have come to consider meals ought to be.

Older Eaters

'It is quite surprising that black treacle
is so seldom recommended as a good cheap source of
nourishment for the old.'

AS LIFE GOES BY every one of us becomes increasingly affected by senility. The word may be associated in your mind with all sorts of horrific images of its extreme effects, but there is no real need for it to alarm you to that extent. Senility just means the business of growing old, and it affects different mechanisms of the body at different ages, and nobody really knows why. A fighter pilot is at his peak at about nineteen; by the time he is twenty-five, he is already past his best. In the main, however, senility only begins after the age of thirty. Up till then, most of the body's systems are at full strength. But after this, the efficiency of the heart as a pump falls away by about 8 per cent each decade so that by the time you're seventy your heart has lost 30 per cent or so of its effectiveness. Your lungs don't pump so well either: you can expect them to work only 60 per cent as well when you are seventy as they did when you were thirty.

As age advances, the nerves convey their messages more slowly, the skin loses its elasticity and the kidneys filter out wastes more sluggishly. And the rate at which the body's machinery 'ticks over' – what scientists call the 'basal metabolic rate' – slows down. At seventy you use up only about 90 per cent of energy doing nothing as you did at thirty. But besides this, a seventy-year-old seldom sprints upstairs two steps at a time, hurries about less and usually does less physically demanding work than a thirty-year-old; that is, he uses up less energy, and therefore needs to eat less.

Moreover, older people tend to dry out. As their skin loses elasticity, it also becomes drier, and indeed the proportion of water in the body as a whole steadily dwindles as age advances. In addition, as people age their sense of thirst, which in their prime they always assumed to be automatic, begins to get out of adjustment, and sometimes fails altogether. When a young man is 'dry', he feels thirsty. An old man may in fact *be* dry, or what the doctors call dehydrated, but not know it and may become really ill.

There are other systems that can go wrong with advancing age. One is the sense of balance. Everybody knows that grandmother is constantly in danger of falling over or, at least, of tripping on the carpet. The sense of cold, too, can fail, with disastrous results. When young healthy people feel cold they shiver: that is, they burn up food to do work (shivering) from which heat is produced to keep their bodies warm. Old people, whose shivering mechanism is out of order, become cold without realising it. Some old people die of cold (hypothermia) because they cannot afford heating; some die because their body machinery does not tell them they are cold.

How Old Are You?

One way of measuring a person's age is to look at his birth certificate. This tells the number of years and months he has lived, and it provides a very simple method of administering an organisation; we can say that at such-and-such an age we will accept you as a worker in a factory, a voter or a married man, and at some other date we shall stop you working, pay you a pension and allow you to travel free on the buses. But a birth certificate can be very inaccurate as a measure of the physical and human state. There are men still full of vigour and drive years after their calendar age compels them to give up work, just as there are those whose powers begin to flag well before they are permitted to stop.

These considerations affect people's need for food. Though the nutritional scientists can say that *on average* a man over fifty-five needs 10 per cent less food to eat than he did at thirty-five, and that at seventy-five he can do as well with 20 per cent less, this may be wide of the mark for a particular individual.

The variations between individual old people are not quite like variations between individual children or between adults in the prime of life : the special characteristic of an old person is the point in time when old age overcomes him. I do not say 'when old age creeps over him'. The change that then takes place is more abrupt than anything that can be described as creeping.

OLD PEOPLE

None of us can escape the gradual loss of skin elasticity, the gentle slowing down of basal metabolism, the weakening of memory or the fading of the sense of balance and the apprehension of heat and cold. Even though people in their sixties are still full of drive and ambition, even though they are still capable of a full day's work, whether manual labour, school-teaching, running a business or running the country, these people are – and there is no use pretending – old. They still have good appetites, and though their needs for energy-value have fallen off, their needs for protein, vitamins and minerals are as great as they ever were. But just like other people, if they continue to eat a varied mixture of wholesome food, which is made easier if they eat cooked meals fairly regularly, they are likely to come to no harm. And they may go on like this for years. But eventually there will come a change. It may come in the fifties, the sixties or the seventies, or it may be postponed to the eighties – and no one really knows why. But when it comes it is often quite abrupt.

VERY OLD PEOPLE

At whatever age the change may come, healthy, vigorous, lively and useful old people suddenly become *very* old. The drive that keeps most of us going for most of our lives dies down, and all at once they are sitting back quite passively in a chair. As the decades pass by, the body suffers a loss of brain cells. They do not appear to die away indiscriminately but, so far as memory is concerned, seem to follow trades union principles of 'last in, first out'. If you have had old grandparents you will know how, while fond of you and their other grandchildren, they tend to forget your name and call you by the name of your mother or father, that is, of their own child. Later they may muddle up your parents' names with those of your great-uncles and great-aunts, who of course were their own brothers and sisters. The oldest memories always last the longest. So that quite often old people cannot remember that they have in fact just finished eating their dinner and can therefore expect the next meal to be supper, not dinner. Or they may forget about eating dinner altogether. And such very old people (like the children that Shakespeare compared them with) cannot be depended upon to select a proper diet for themselves.

Many old people, as they become very old, gradually shrivel up. In extreme old age, as the heart's capacity to pump blood diminishes and the ability to maintain the body's temperature begins to break down, nature seems to compensate for these losses by seeing to it that the frail old person has less body for the weakening system to keep going. If, therefore, as you help to put your old, old grandmother to bed you notice that she is little more than skin and bone, don't imagine that you have been starving her. You must go on taking care that she *does* get all she needs to eat, because she can no longer take care of herself, but in this last stage of life (as in the first) there are special nutritional needs.

Where to be Watchful

As the first stage of ageing merges into the second 'very old' stage, there are four things to watch for.

How much to eat?

Though the total amount of food requirements becomes less, it is important to make sure that the old person is not prevented from getting enough by being unable to go out to the shops, by being too poor to buy food, by being able to cook or by being too forgetful. On the other hand, while there are comparatively few fat old men, because most fat men die before they become old, it is good sense to discourage old people from eating more than they need and becoming obese, just as it is for anyone else.

Vegetables and fruit

There are three good reasons for making sure that old people eat enough vegetables and fruit. The first is that eating these foods ensures that they get enough *vitamin C*. Although this vegetable-and-orange-juice vitamin is good for health, it is uncommon to find actual illness due to its lack, except among very poor incompetent people (or drunks in skid row). But old people do suffer from anaemia more often than younger people do; and the second reason to make sure that they eat vegetables is that greens and the like provide *folic acid* which is concerned with preventing anaemia. The third reason, while not yet a scientific certainty, is that they're going to run short of *potassium*. Some old people who had appeared completely gaga have turned out merely to be short of potassium, which is also contained in potatoes and green vegetables. When their supplies of this were topped up, they became as bright as a button again.

A note about potassium. Potassium chloride is a substance rather like common salt, which is in scientific terms the chemical sodium chloride. We know quite well that salt is circulating through our bodies because, if our noses bleed, the blood running into our mouths is salty. And when we sweat, the sweat is salty too. But potassium chloride is held *inside* our blood cells and the other cells of the body. Ordinary people hardly ever run short of potassium, which is why nutritional scientists rarely bother about it. But if they do they become mentally confused, and they also suffer from muscular weakness. People lose potassium when they suffer from certain wasting diseases, or when they waste after a serious operation. Though old age is not an illness, any more than infancy is, people's bodies undoubtedly waste as their age advances. Since loss of potassium accompanies wasting, it is prudent to see that ageing people get their potassium by eating those vegetables that contain it.

MEAT

If old men and women were unable to behave at mealtimes like the middle-aged people they once were, meat would not need to be singled out as something to take special care about. But when people become old they may gradually give up eating meat for two reasons. The first is that it can become a nuisance for them to eat as the shapes of their mouths change and their false teeth fit more loosely. And the other reason is that they may become unable to afford to buy it. All the same, anaemia due to a shortage of iron is more common in old people than it ought to be. Meat is a good source of iron, and there is just as much in cheap mince as there is in a steak or a chop, while liver is probably the best iron source of all.

There is one source of iron (and of potassium too) which is cheaper than meat. It is quite surprising that *black treacle* is so seldom recommended as a good cheap source of nourishment for the old. True, you can't eat it, as you can meat, a quarter of a pound at a sitting. But a spoonful or so each day will provide these minerals in a form that is tasty and easy to eat.

FOOD FOR OLD BONES

One of the main components of bone is calcium. A well-fed young child absorbs calcium from his food quickly enough to remake his bones completely (and make them grow) within one or two years. By the time he is fully grown, however, although he is still taking in calcium from food and making his bones become stronger and more solid, it is absorbed more slowly and his bones get fully remade only after ten or twelve years. By the time he reaches middle age, his bones are beginning actually to lose calcium. And from then on, as his hair turns grey, his eyes become long-sighted and all the other marks of ageing affect his body and the rate at which his bones lose calcium and become weaker accelerates.

Some old people lose calcium from their bones more quickly than others do; no one fully understands why. But when people become really old (at whatever age it happens) they become literally frail: that is to say, *they are breakable.* An old lady steps off the kerb; perhaps because she is not looking where she is going, she goes down with a bump and breaks her thigh bone, even though the fall was quite trivial.

The question is whether the kind of food old people eat has anything to do with the rate at which they lose calcium and the age at which their bones become dangerously fragile. Sadly, I must reply that, so far as we can tell from the scientific knowledge that we have at present, it does not. While there is probably no harm in persuading old people to drink milk and eat cheese, or to take cod-liver oil, there is no firm evidence that it does them any good.

On the other hand, it is quite clear that exercise is an important factor in holding back the loss of calcium. There is some truth in the old joke about the man who considered it dangerous to go to bed because he had observed that more people die in bed than anywhere else. One of the most striking results of a long stay in bed (which may be

necessary for patients with certain diseases or injuries) is
that quite soon calcium begins to leak away from the bones.
Indeed, a loss of calcium has been observed even in fit
young men who have been kept lying down in a space
capsule for only a few weeks, which is why astronauts are
now required to carry out vigorous physical exercises.

If a forty-year-old wants to hang on to calcium in middle
age so as to arrive at old age with as good a supply as can be
managed, the best thing to do is to be physically active.
And there is no doubt that the most effective policy for
preserving old bones is to be active too. Unless there is
some good reason for your aged grandmother to stay in
bed, there are even better reasons why she should be up
and about for as long as she can. One is so that she may keep
the calcium in her bones. Another is that by so doing she
stands a better chance of keeping her appetite and thus
being able to enjoy her meals and to eat a good balanced
diet.

Meals for Old People

Contrary to popular belief, old people's digestions are
usually as good as ever they were. After all, as long as they
are still in the first stage of old age, when they are still spry
and busy, they can still be categorised with working
people. Our community is foolish when it arbitrarily tells a
man of sixty-five, or a woman of sixty, that they are 'old' –
and ridiculous in telling a woman she is old five years
before her twin brother, when one of the most striking
differences between the sexes is that women are tougher
and more durable. In other societies, old women are
expected to go on working as useful citizens at an age when
we would pension them off and condemn them to spend
their days on subsidised bus tours.

The first nutritional rule for old people's diets is to give
them the same *variety of foods* as anyone else would expect.

The second rule is that *they should not be fed on slops*, just because their teeth do not fit properly, or because they have become clumsy, knock things over and spill food on themselves. Babies can live on milk for a few weeks because they are born with a good supply of iron and vitamins. Things are quite different for old people. During a long life they may from time to time have neglected to eat enough or perhaps not understood the importance of ringing the changes – from sandwiches to Irish stew, from fish and chips to steak and onions – that is, their diet has not been as good as it should have been. If so, they may come to old age with low reserves of iron and vitamins. They face the future already nutritionally 'overdrawn', whereas infants come into the world with a 'balance in the bank'.

The third rule is to make sure that a changing mixture of foods as the seasons go by is presented to old people *in a form with which they can cope*. If Granny can no longer cut up her meat for herself, she needs someone to do it for her, doesn't she? Nutrition is about this, just as much as it is about proteins, carbohydrates and vitamins.

'Meals on Wheels'

With all our care and attention for the public health of the nation, for the quality of the national diet and its freedom from toxic contaminants, we have given signally little concern to love and companionship, especially for the old. While some families are prepared to have a grandparent living with them, many more either won't or can't. Nor do the nutritional scientists often emphasise the importance of their doing so. There are good arguments for spending money on adding vitamins to bread and to margarine, but there are better arguments for trying to arrange affairs so that, just as a young baby is expected to have a mother to look after it and feed it at the beginning of its life, an old person should have a child to do the same at the end.

Just as our society provides nutrition for babies who have no readily available mothers, so too it does for old people with no accessible children. Two nutritional principles lie behind the idea of the 'meals on wheels' that are brought to old and frail people in their own homes.

The first principle is *to complete the mixture*. It is assumed that old people are able to provide a breakfast for themselves of tea with bread and butter (or margarine, which is nowadays almost its exact equivalent). And for an evening meal old people, even if they are poor and find it difficult to do much shopping or cooking, will eat bread and cheese and perhaps cake, together with anything left over from lunch. But if it can be taken that there is enough to eat, it may be hard for them to have a wide enough mixture. The carried-in meal, therefore, should provide potatoes and fresh vegetables, the articles most likely to be missing from the old people's menus, and also meat (or chicken, fish, liver or kidney).

The second principle is *to make the diet more agreeable*. If pensioners are short of money and, above all, cannot exert the effort needed to prepare and cook a varied meal, they can easily fall into a routine of eating the same thing every day. This may lead to their not eating enough because the tedious repetition becomes uninspiring, and to a mono-tonous, unvarying diet that can even produce outright malnutrition.

WHEN 'MEALS' NEED CARE

What happens to the vitamin C? When you cook yourself a potato, turn it out of the saucepan and eat it straight away, you get some vitamin C. The same holds good when you cook some cabbage – as long as you don't cook it to death. Undoubtedly, some vitamin C is lost during the cooking but this does not imply that an old lady would necessarily do better if she ate her cabbage raw. For one thing, a reasonable helping of raw shredded cabbage almost always contains less cabbage than a helping of boiled cabbage served up as part of that well-balanced and popular combination, 'meat and two veg'. Another objection is that old people often don't like raw cabbage and the third is that they may have difficulty in chewing it up.

The nutritional problem with 'meals on wheels' comes from the 'wheels' part of the operation. In order to deliver the meals in a tasty and acceptable condition, they have to be kept hot. There is no nutritional value in hotness but people like hot meals to be hot and steaming and complain if they are not – indeed, they may even refuse to eat them if they are stone-cold. Unfortunately, keeping food hot is a very effective way of destroying the vitamin C in it. The longer it is kept hot, the less vitamin C lands up on people's plates.

Old people need tempting. Of course, 'meals on wheels' must be made up of a proper variety of nourishing foods. But it is equally important that they should be well cooked and attractively presented. Sometimes, when plates are piled one on top of the other on metal collars while they are in a van, a brown ring of gravy dries on to the lower plates. This doesn't affect the vitamins in the potatoes, but it doesn't look very nice. And when food does not look nice, people are reluctant to eat it.

Or the food may not be brought round to the old people on a plate at all. It may come in a 'mess tin' or some other container. The driver who brings it round may be in a hurry. The result can be that the food, nourishing though it may be, gets ladled out all muddled up together. Part of the value of 'meals on wheels' and part of the benefit which they are designed to achieve will be lost if the result of all this is that they are not attractive to people.

Most Important Deficiency

To sum up, the food an old person needs to be well fed is in the main not much different from what anyone else requires. As people get older they need less to eat. But they need the same mixture, including some meat, eggs, fish or chicken, some potatoes, greens and fruit, some milk and cheese, and some bread and butter, rice pudding, cake and cornflakes.

Good company, however, is the most important ingredient of a good meal; one of the most horrible punishments imaginable is prolonged solitary confinement. All too often, however, old people have no company at all, good or bad, at mealtimes. The most serious nutritional deficiency for old people, far worse than overcooked greens that could lead to a lack of vitamin C or a shortage of meat capable of causing anaemia, is a *deficiency of love*. The old may be dribbling and forgetful; nevertheless the best way to keep their diet right is companionship. Just as the senses of thirst, balance, heat and cold all weaken as age advances, so do the pangs of hunger. A friend, a visitor, a daughter or a grandchild to talk to at teatime can be worth an entire chemist's shopful of vitamins! As old people become really old – as they pass from old age to very old age – what needs watching most closely is whether they have company. They will be lonely enough when they die; it is worth making an effort to prevent them from being lonely before then.

FIVE

Illness

'. . . broad beans and chocolate are also thought
to contain substances that produce headaches
in some people.'

THERE ARE ILLNESSES which from their very nature, compel people to change their diet: to avoid certain foods or food ingredients, or to eat more of some foods and less of others. People who are very unwell may be unable or unwilling to eat at all. In the main, however, illness does not affect a person's nutritional requirements. If serious injury or illness makes it necessary radically to limit the sufferer's diet for a time, this restricted diet must not be continued for too long. In the past, people did themselves considerable harm through believing that they ought not to eat this or that while they were ill, or that they should live only on slops or on some fancy confection. Limiting the patient's diet like this could *produce* malnutrition on top of the disease that made him ill in the first place.

Constipation

The best way to treat most constipation is *not* to worry about missing a daily stool now and then and certainly *not* to start taking laxatives and believing the persuasive advertisements of the laxative manufacturers, but to take a few common-sense steps to help the situation.

☐ It is helpful to follow a consistent *routine* of going to the lavatory at a set time each day, usually after breakfast. Parents do their children a good turn if they train them to adopt such a regular habit. Certainly, they should not allow them to break their routine from mere laziness.

☐ Regular *exercise* will also help, especially for people whose life is predominantly sedentary.

☐ Evidence about the nutritional benefit of *roughage* – sometimes called fibre or bulk – is certainly not as straightforward as those who crusade on its behalf would lead their listeners to imagine. For people who are troubled by constipation, however, it is good practice gradually to increase the amount of roughage they eat, in the form of wholemeal bread, fruit, cabbage and other green vegetables, or breakfast cereals containing bran.

☐ Finally, it can be useful to drink a tumblerful of *warm water* first thing in the morning, another glass of water during the day and yet another last thing at night.

Note. All this applies to the everyday constipation which almost everyone experiences now and then. If the condition is prolonged and severe, however, the sufferer should consult a doctor.

'Feed a Cold: Starve a Fever'

This saying belongs to past history and has little bearing on the nutrition of sick people nowadays.

COLDS

Colds are a nuisance, but usually little more. There is at present no known scientific method of cure or treatment, but luckily almost everyone gets well again quite quickly, whether the cold is 'treated' or not. It thus seems reasonable to go on eating a full, properly chosen diet when you have a cold. If you have been eating a bad diet beforehand (lacking in vegetables, perhaps, or butter) then clearly the sooner this is put right the better; but this advice applies equally whether you have a cold or not. A glass of hot milk before going to bed may be useful if you have previously been scamping your food; a glass of hot whisky is also recommended by some people. But neither whisky nor milk has been proved to have any significant effect on cold viruses. The main reason for taking one or the other is that it can make you feel better, and that is something gained in the wait for the cold to go away of itself.

FEVERS

Before the science of medicine took over from the art of healing, a fever could be a serious and a long-drawn-out affair. Today, with the help of potent antibiotics and other drugs, few people have to suffer from high fever for long.

While fever lasts, however, the main thing is to save the patient from needing to make any exertion in consuming and digesting food. Warm milk, perhaps with an egg beaten into it, or maybe a fruit drink such as crushed orange with a little sugar, are all that he will want to take.

This is not exactly 'starving a fever', but is the sort of thing to provide while high fever lasts. As soon as the patient's temperature goes down to normal, however, the diet should gradually be restored and a proper, varied mixture of foods again provided.

Food Poisoning

The most important thing about food poisoning is how not to get it, and this I have discussed in Chapter 2. But if you are unlucky enough to succumb to a bad bout of food poisoning with severe diarrhoea, you may wonder what is best to eat while you have got it. The answer is: nothing. But once the worst is over – and most attacks subside within 48 hours – or if the attack is not too severe, the best foods to eat are those which are easy to take. Milk ranks high, together with such milky foods as junket, custard and yogurt. As you begin to feel better, you should gradually return to an adequate mixed diet although for a while you should avoid coarse fibrous foods – cabbage, wholemeal bread and, of course, bran. More important than food, however, is drink which is needed to replace the liquid lost through diarrhoea. Water by itself is useful, or a little salt can be added to it. Alternatively, a simple fruit drink such as orangeade or lemonade may be more acceptable.

While food poisoning, although disagreeable, is usually little more than a nuisance, sometimes it is more serious and must then be treated with respect. For example, violent attacks can prostrate the sufferer and call for medical attention. Paratyphoid is a highly infectious type of food poisoning, and while it may not be particularly distressing, it must be treated seriously for fear of its spreading, and sufferers are usually sent to hospital and isolated until they are free from infection. Typhoid is far less serious now that it can be quickly and effectively treated by antibiotics, but it also involves instant isolation.

Headache

Headaches have dozens of different causes. If you suffer from persistent headaches, you should go to your doctor, but occasional headaches can easily be as puzzling to doctors as they are to you. Most headaches have nothing to do with your food, but there are some exceptions.

Constipation. Bouts of constipation are sometimes associated with a feeling of 'heaviness' often accompanied by headache. It is therefore sensible to take account of the advice given at the beginning of this chapter on avoiding constipation.

Pickled herrings, cheese and chocolate. Although the scientific evidence is by no means conclusive, *some* headaches appear to be caused for *some* people by compounds called 'pressor amines' which occur naturally in certain foods, especially in pickled herrings, yeast extracts like Marmite, and some Cheddar cheeses. Some other cheeses (Stilton, Emmental and Brie), some red wines and avocado pears may also contain appreciable quantities. And broad beans and chocolate are also thought to contain substances that produce headaches in some people.

If, therefore, you suffer now and then from unaccountable headaches, try to remember whether this follows your having eaten one or other of these foods. If so, it is obviously sensible to see whether giving up such foods has any effect on freeing you from headaches in the future.

High Blood Pressure

Some people gradually develop high blood pressure later in life and some do not, but the reasons for these differences are not known. So you cannot tell whether your blood pressure is likely to rise seriously as you get older. There are two ways, however, in which your diet can affect your blood pressure:

☐ *Being overweight.* There is a marked tendency for corpulence to be associated with high blood pressure. So if, as you get older, your blood pressure tends to rise there is even more reason why you should take the steps to keep your weight down that you ought to have taken anyway.

☐ *Eating salt.* Salt is a necessary component of a good diet, and of good cooking. On the other hand, a great many people eat more salt than they need, just because they like the taste and not because they have any particular requirement for it. Now it has been shown that blood pressure that has become too high can be reduced if a diet low in salt is adopted. It follows, therefore, that those with a tendency to high blood pressure should avoid taking too much salt. Those who cook for them should go easy on salt in the kitchen, and on baking soda too. This implies cutting down on foods which contain a good deal of salt, such as bacon and ham, sausages, canned meat, cheese and, of course, kippers and other cured fish. Salt is used in making bread and biscuits as well, and in other ready-made products such as baked beans, sandwich spreads or soup mixes, so these foods should be used sparingly, or else prepared at home with only the minimum of salt. And of course such people should avoid adding extra salt when the food comes to the table.

Peptic Ulcers

The term 'peptic ulcer' covers both gastric ulcers (in the stomach) and duodenal ulcers (further along the gut in the duodenum). It is an example of how wonderfully made we are that more of us do *not* have ulcers. After all, most people have no difficulty in digesting tough meat without digesting their own stomachs, though the reasons why we can do this are by no means completely understood. So perhaps we ought not to be surprised that certain people *do* digest at least odd spots of their own stomachs and duodenums, because that is what peptic ulcers are – holes digested through the wall of the gut itself.

Not long ago, the accepted treatment for a peptic ulcer was to restrict severely the amount and the variety of foods the patient ate. Later it was discovered that this did no good; on the contrary, patients were often found to be actually starving themselves, or showing symptoms of vitamin deficiency. Nowadays the advice given to people with ulcers is different.

First, they should, with due prudence, eat the meals they like and make sure that they eat the varied mixture of foods which is the most important basis of good nutrition.

Secondly, they should avoid eating big meals but take their food as a series of small meals and snacks eaten at regular intervals and, as nearly as can be managed, at the same times each day.

Third, during any period of discomfort, they should avoid irritants such as alcohol, strong tea or coffee, cola drinks, and highly seasoned items like Bovril, Oxo or

Marmite, bacon, salt fish and curry. Coarse, fibrous foods like bran and wholemeal bread should also be avoided, as well as nuts, currants and raisins, the pips and skins of fruit, onions, radishes, celery and raw cabbage. In addition, while they – like everybody else – should have vegetables, fruit and fruit-juice, it is a good idea to sieve their fruit and vegetables after they have been cooked in order to take out any pieces of skin and stalk.

It is only common sense for ulcer sufferers not to irritate their ulcers by drinking their tea or eating their food too hot. It is also sensible for them not to gobble their food or hurry over their meals but to eat them in a leisurely and harmonious manner in good company. But this advice applies also to those of us without ulcers, doesn't it?

Gout

Gout is no laughing matter. Suddenly to wake up in the night with an excruciating pain, usually in the big toe, can be an unnerving experience. Moreover, gout is more common than many people imagine; in most western countries, about 3 per cent of all the men over thirty have attacks of gout at one time or another. And gout tends to run in families. If your father or your uncle suffers from gout, therefore, you would be prudent to pay close attention to the following paragraphs.

Gout is due to a gritty accumulation of crystals of uric acid in a joint, which act to prevent it from moving smoothly – hence the agonising pain. Gout can effectively be treated by several different drugs, one of which is romantically enough prepared from the autumn crocus. Just the same, it is better so to arrange one's life as not to have an attack at all.

☐ Obviously, if you are likely to be susceptible – that is to say, if you are a man, over thirty, belonging to a family in which a male relative or ancestor has had gout – it is sensible for you to avoid foods which are particularly rich in the compounds from which uric acid is derived in the body. These include sweetbreads, liver, kidneys, and yeast extract and products that contain it, such as packeted gravy.

☐ Men who are overweight are more susceptible to gout than those who are not. If you belong to a gouty family, therefore, it is particularly important not to allow yourself to get fat. On the other hand, once you know that you can have gout (by having had an attack), you should organise your slimming regime gently. Starving yourself in an effort to lose weight quickly may bring on a recurrence.

☐ Port wine was once held to be particularly dangerous to gouty men. It is now known that too much alcohol from any source predisposes one to an attack.

☐ A big meal such as a banquet, a Christmas party or a reunion dinner may also bring on an attack.

Gout is, unfortunately for them, a disease of men. Women *can* contract gout but only one woman suffers for every eight men. The ancient Greeks observed that eunuchs never had gout; a discussion of this point, however, hardly falls within the ambit of a book about nutrition.

Kidney Stones

Luckily, far fewer people suffer from kidney stones, or 'renal calculi' as they are also called, than in historical times although in parts of the world, mainly in the tropics, the complaint is still quite common. At one time boys and young men used to suffer from stones but nowadays they are most common in older men. There are several varieties of stones (or gravel as they are called when they take the form of numerous small particles collecting in the bladder). Some of these are composed primarily of uric acid so that men with a tendency to gout may be particularly susceptible. If you have a tendency to kidney stones, you should drink plenty of fluid, particularly just before you go to bed, and you should avoid eating sweetbreads, kidneys, liver and products containing yeast extract.

A substance called oxalic acid is connected with another kind of stone. Men susceptible to these should avoid eating foods rich in oxalates such as rhubarb or spinach and would also be wise to cut down on tea or coffee.

Food Allergy

Some people regularly become ill after eating a particular food. These people are said to be *allergic* to whatever food it is, or to possess an *allergy* to the food. All sorts of foods have been incriminated, including eggs, milk (usually cows' milk), wheat flour (which also involves bread, cake, biscuits and anything else made with flour) and many others which are perfectly nourishing and agreeable to most people : strawberries, broad beans, sardines, shellfish, all sorts of meat including beef, mutton and pork, nuts of various kinds, mustard, mushrooms, tomatoes, celery, chocolate, oranges, the cooking of certain Chinese restaurants – indeed, there is hardly a food that someone somewhere is not allergic to.

An allergy may show up in various ways. Sometimes the symptoms are comparatively slight and amount to little more than a nuisance. Sometimes they may be very severe, prostrating the sufferer or even leading to his death. What happens usually falls into one of the following seven categories :

☐ *Skin.* Nettle-rash or hives may appear or there may be swelling or reddening of the skin with eczema.

☐ *Breathing*. Food allergy may show itself as hay-fever or asthma.

☐ *Circulation*. A sufferer may actually collapse from shock.

☐ *Headache*. The connection between headache and certain articles of food has been discussed earlier in this chapter.

☐ *Digestive system*. Food allergy can cause indigestion, vomiting, stomach-ache or diarrhoea.

☐ *Dark-coloured urine*. This may be due to red colouring from the blood getting into the urine.

☐ *Pain in the joints*. Occasionally a food allergy may cause a sufferer's joints to become swollen and painful.

The way to treat an allergy to a particular food is to stop eating the food that causes the trouble. This sounds simple, but it may be more difficult than it seems.

First of all, it may not be easy to identify the food in question. A headache, for example, *may* be due to an allergic reaction to cheese but this may be difficult to prove if it does not come on immediately after the cheese is eaten. Headaches (like any other symptoms of allergy) may also be due to causes quite unconnected with food. Sometimes, however, people get it into their heads that some food or other disagrees with them and – let us say – brings them out in a rash, maybe because once upon a time they had a rash immediately after eating, say, margarine, without any adequate evidence that margarine actually had anything to do with the matter. And for years and years afterwards they go on, quite unnecessarily, avoiding margarine. Before making up your mind, therefore, it is a good idea to arrange a trial by, for example, eating cake without knowing whether or not margarine has been included in the recipe. It is sensible to repeat a trial of this sort several times before deciding to consider the connection between the food and the allergy as proved. (Naturally, if the reaction to a particular food is clear and serious, a 'blind' test of this sort should never be carried out; you might do grave harm.)

A second problem arises when allergies appear in infants and children, as they often do. Obviously, if an allergy is due to wheat flour or milk it will be difficult to organise a nutritious diet that completely omits the offending article. Some young children have a serious condition called coeliac disease which is a reaction against wheat protein. In dealing with this, elaborate arrangements have to be made over many years to ensure that the child eats no wheat products at all; cornflour, for instance, is used to replace wheat flour. When the child's allergy is for cows' milk, it is sometimes possible to substitute goats' milk.

Very often, people grow out of their allergies. If your allergy is merely to peanuts, let us say, it is very little trouble to ensure that you eat a good mixed diet without ever coming near a peanut. But if you are allergic to a staple food there is always a danger that in steering clear of it you may not give yourself enough to eat. If your allergy is gradually fading as the years go by then of course the sooner you know about it and can resume a normal diet the better. It is, therefore, good practice every now and then to check up and see whether you are still sensitive to a small amount of whatever it was that once brought on your symptoms.

Diabetes

People keep going because the food they eat supplies them with fuel in the form of glucose which circulates in their blood. The way the concentration of glucose is controlled in the blood of healthy people is quite complicated, because extra fuel supplies have to be made available automatically when heavy muscular activity begins and the supply has then to be cut back automatically when the physical effort stops. In a person who has diabetes this control is upset so that, after eating a meal, particularly if it contains sugary or starchy foods, the amount of glucose in the blood rises uncontrollably. The situation can be compared to a car. When you need to go faster, you step on the accelerator and more petrol goes into the engine; when you slow down the increased flow of petrol stops. Diabetes can roughly be compared with having the choke kept open throughout the journey so that the engine is flooded with petrol and cannot operate properly.

It has been estimated that up to half a million people in Great Britain suffer, either slightly or severely, from diabetes. Although children and young people may contract it, most diabetics are over fifty. More boys than girls have diabetes, but among middle-aged people more women suffer from the disease than men.

No one knows exactly what causes diabetes, but there is some evidence that, at least to some extent, it runs in families. It does not follow, however, that because a parent or another blood relative has been a sufferer, a child will develop diabetes either early or later in life. But there is certainly a connection between diabetes and obesity: people who have allowed themselves to become overweight are more susceptible to diabetes than thin people. Since obesity also tends to run in families, it is sensible for people to take particular care if they belong to a thick-set family.

In addition, diabetes is to some degree related to good living: people who keep 'a good table', are fond of good eating and have a 'sweet tooth' – *and* indulge their liking for sugary things – are more likely to contract diabetes than those who live more frugally, though why this is so is by no means clear.

Diabetes has sometimes been found to develop in people who have suffered from a severe infectious disease or an injury. Emotional distress has also been thought to bring it on and pregnancy too can be the prelude to diabetes, especially in women who have had several children.

Not so long ago, diabetes was a fatal disease quickly leading to coma and death. Those with a mild form of the disease were condemned for life to a rigidly controlled diet. Nowadays, a diabetic can live quite normally provided he attends to two things.

First of all, the doctor who has diagnosed the disease will assess how severe his diabetes is, and will then prescribe a certain regular dose of insulin. Though a healthy body produces its own insulin automatically in the exact amount needed to control the quantity of glucose that is circulating in the blood at the time, a diabetic has to take insulin each day, in amounts which can deal with his particular average daily needs.

Next, in order that such average conditions are reasonably well maintained the diabetic must arrange his diet to provide approximately the same amounts of sugars and other carbohydrates, of protein and of fat each day. This *could* be done if he ate exactly the same meals every day, but since this would be intolerably monotonous, he must learn how to swop different items about to give himself a change of menu without changing the amounts of the different dietary ingredients. Most sensible diabetics who can be trusted to do their sums properly are given a set of tables showing how to exchange one food for another without upsetting the balance of the diet. For example, in terms of *carbohydrate*, an ounce of jam is equivalent to $1\frac{1}{2}$ oz of cornflakes, 6 oz of banana or 12 oz of raw apple. In terms of *protein*, 2 oz of lean meat are equivalent to the same amount of cheese, 3 oz of fish or nearly 10 oz of milk. And in terms of *fat*, an ounce of lard equals $1\frac{1}{2}$ oz of butter, 2 oz of mayonnaise or 6 oz of cream.

Cancer

The normal wholesome food that ordinary people eat has

no connection with cancer. Sufferers should therefore eat so far as they are able the same nourishing diet that everyone else requires. Nor are there any foods that are known to cause cancer or to be capable of harming someone thought to be susceptible to the disease. Obviously, if there was any scientific evidence that one food or another caused cancer, such an item would not be permitted to be sold. The results of some research in the United States, however, suggest – I can put it no higher – that obese women who eat a lot of fat *may* be somewhat more likely to contract breast cancer than those who eat less rich food and who are not overweight. Certain cancers of the intestines may also attack corpulent people more often than those who are the right weight for their height. Other researchers, too, seem to be obtaining results suggesting that if people eat a rich diet containing a high proportion of meat and fat and thus a low proportion of cereal products such as, in particular, bread, they may become somewhat more susceptible to cancer of the bowel.

This chapter has shown that there are certain diseases that are more or less directly affected by diet and nutrition. Others, which I have mentioned elsewhere in this book, include coronary heart disease, which especially in men is related to overeating and to eating too much meat fat and butter, and also anaemia due to lack of iron in the diet. Once I might have written about rickets in babies and young children, but nowadays this is rare in countries like Great Britain or the United States, since sensible mothers see to it that they themselves get their vitamins from the clinic when they are pregnant and that later on their babies do so too. In very poor developing countries, diseases due to other deficiencies are seen – beriberi and pellagra, for instance – but fortunately citizens of prosperous industrial communities never have to deal with these.

By far the most common nutritional disorder in these communities, as well as being the most dangerous, is obesity. Even if it is not quite fair to call it a disease it is, as you will have noticed, connected with heart disease, diabetes, gout, high blood pressure and – just possibly – with cancer as well, besides which it undoubtedly shortens people's lives. If you are seriously interested in good nutrition for yourself and your family, you cannot afford to disregard the hazards it presents.

Foods and Fads

'... farmers who want dark yellow yolks to their battery eggs
can, and do, easily make them so by including carotene
in the birds' diet.'

WHEN YOU APPROACH the subject of nutrition, *don't* leave your common sense behind. Your common sense should tell you that although some scientific discoveries have clearly improved things that were obviously wrong, very few discoveries have improved things that had very little wrong with them in the first place. In other words, *don't* lose your nerve in the face of some of the more remarkable allegations about what is supposed to be good for you (for example, sea-salt crystals or raw carrots) and what is said to be harmful (like white bread or baked beans on toast).

Important scientific discoveries stand out and can easily be recognised and understood. In medicine, there were the discoveries that stopped people from dying of smallpox and diphtheria and that led to the closing down of the tuberculosis hospitals for lack of patients. Although too many men in the prime of life still die of heart disease, we are beginning to understand how diet can help to remedy the situation. It is common sense to take note of such discoveries. But it is nonsense to wake up one morning in what is, with all its minor troubles, a well-fed community and believe the morning newspaper's report that white bread, which millions of perfectly healthy people have eaten all their lives, is 'poison', or that battery eggs do no one any good. Far too many of these wild statements are flying about, and we should look at them closely in the clear, cold light of common sense.

'Health Foods'

The term 'health foods' is misleading. It implies that foods that are not 'health foods' and that are not bought (often rather expensively) from a 'health food' shop are 'ill-health foods'. This is just not true. Many people like the taste of coarse bread made from stone-ground wholemeal flour, and there is nothing wrong with that. Others like the idea of eating something similar to the simple food they believe (without much justification) their ancestors ate in the supposedly pure and innocent days of long ago. There is nothing wrong with that either. People's tastes differ. What *is* wrong, however, is to believe that eating such foods – and paying extra money for them – will in some way improve your health. And it is even worse to accuse people who are perfectly happy eating an ordinary everyday diet of being not only foolish but wicked as well.

Besides harmless, if costly, 'health foods', however, many so-called 'health food' shops also sell 'nonsense' articles that purport to cure this disease or prevent that – tablets and pills, nostrums and powders, seaweed extracts and exotic apple concentrates. The claims put forward for many of these are quite groundless. Not only do they cost money, and not only do they not fulfil the promises made on their behalf, but they also mislead people about the real nature of nutritional science, especially as to what it can do for health and what it cannot. There is *no* food which will fill you with ebullient health whenever you are feeling gloomy.

Brown Bread or White?

You have only got to look at white bread and brown bread to know that their compositions are different. But what you want to know is: is one better for you than the other?

The short answer is that normally there is nothing to choose between them. The main reason for selecting one kind of bread rather than another is that you like it better. In western countries, most people choose to eat white bread. The nonsense comes in when people develop a passion for brown bread as if it were a matter of religion, and not only eat it with enthusiasm themselves but fervently attack those who do not as though to touch sliced white bread, besides damaging the health, was tantamount to mortal sin. The first shot in the campaign is usually to compare white bread to cotton wool, a harmless substance which the very comparison implies that they have never eaten.

The *facts* are these: the outer parts of the wheat grain which make brown bread brown – the husk and the embryo – contain more of the B-vitamins, more iron, more fat and more fibre than the rest of the grain. Certainly, if your diet as a whole were lacking in these things, brown bread would be better for you than white bread. But in reasonably prosperous countries, hardly anyone's diet is deficient in B-vitamins, while the iron in brown bread is probably not absorbed by the body at all and the present understanding about fibre is so uncertain that no serious scientist could properly assert that the extra fibre serves any really useful purpose. On the other hand, the extra fat in brown flour makes it keep less well than white, and the extra fibre can actually subtract from the minerals – iron, calcium and zinc – that you get from the rest of your food.

In short, whether you choose to eat white or brown bread is a matter of taste and emotion rather than a question of nourishment.

The Egg Controversy

This is another topic upon which people become emotional but which is in fact a matter of taste; it usually turns upon the question of the colour of an egg's shell. Brown is once again assumed to be a sign of quality and white a sign of inferiority. In fact, the colour of the eggshell has nothing to do with the way the hen is housed or fed but, like the colour of her feathers or of your skin, is solely a matter of race. There is no measurable difference in the chemical composition or nutritional value of brown eggs and white eggs.

Nor does the way laying hens are managed make much difference to the composition of their eggs. Where there is a difference, it can just as well be in favour of the 'battery' eggs as of their rivals. At one time, the yolks of free-range eggs used to be darker yellow than those of eggs laid by battery hens. The yellowness comes from a pigment (carotene) derived from green leaves, and the difference arose because the birds outside ate more greenstuff than those kept inside. There is no particular nutritional virtue in this yellowness, except that carotene acts as vitamin A. But vitamin A itself is not yellow, and the colour is of no significance if the ration of the battery birds contains ample vitamin A – as it probably does. Nowadays, however, farmers who want dark yellow yolks to their battery eggs can, and do, easily make them so by including carotene in the birds' diet.

The question of the humanity – or otherwise – of keeping hens closely confined in battery units is one that does not concern nutritional science as such, though nutritional scientists as individuals may well hold strong opinions on the subject.

Honey – Is It Magic?

Honey is a very agreeable sticky mixture of sugars to spread on bread and butter. At one time it was virtually the only sweetening agent available to ordinary people and it was therefore prized for its taste. The reason why most people enjoy a sweet taste is unknown – but they do. Some people do so more than others, but their 'sweet tooth' seems to have no connection with their health or with any particular need for sugar.

Honey appears to many people to be an almost magical foodstuff – who would guess that a bee, bumbling round among the flowers, would ever regurgitate so delicious a substance and store it so tidily in little hexagonal pigeon-holes in a honeycomb? – and it has, from time to time, been credited with magical properties. In fact, it is no more nourishing than the humble golden syrup. And what nourishment it does contribute comes solely from its sugar content. The believers in the mysterious beneficial qualities of honey sometimes quote figures for the vitamins or the protein they claim it contains. Such reliable analyses as *are* available, however, indicate the presence of only insignificant traces of these substances, which come only from the contaminants that the bees – which, after all, do the best they can – have left in the honey. The honey's flavour, which is indeed enticing to many people, is due to substances present in even more minute traces.

If you like it, eat it. But don't pay good money for it in the belief that it is a magical medicine or a wonder food. It isn't.

A Good Word for Molasses

Molasses, or 'black treacle', is the thick sticky 'mother liquor' left behind in the process of sugar manufacture after the sugar itself has been made to crystallise and has been separated for its final purification. Every now and then, molasses is put forward by dietary enthusiasts as being particularly good for the health. But molasses is simply a syrupy liquid containing about 50 per cent of sugar, which some people enjoy when it is either spread on bread and butter or incorporated in treacle pudding. But though no cure-all, molasses has its good points.

The syrup from which sugar – and molasses – is obtained is made by crushing sugar cane or sugar beet and washing out the sugar juice with water. This is followed by a long process of boiling the resulting sweet watery solution until eventually the sugar crystallises out, during which a considerable amount of iron is picked up by the liquor from the boiling vats and pipes and remains in the molasses. And this is why molasses can be useful to people who suffer from anaemia due to a lack of iron (see page 64); it is a useful potassium source as well.

Paying for a Crunch

Everyone needs salt; but most people get as much as they need and perhaps more without having to worry about it. Salt occurs naturally in a number of foods, and it is incorporated in others, such as butter, cheese, kippers and bacon, during the process of their manufacture, and bakers also add salt to their dough. People put salt on the side of their plates, not because they have any nutritional need for it, but because they have come, through use and custom, to enjoy the taste of extra salt as a condiment.

Some health-food addicts believe that 'natural' sea salt – usually sold in the form of biggish granules – possess some special nutritional advantage over ordinary supermarket salt. This is certainly not so in those places where the table salt has iodine added to it. Sea salt may taste different from ordinary cheap salt because it contains other things besides what is generally known as salt, namely sodium chloride. These other components, however, are of no known nutritional value, though they may contribute a tang which purchasers enjoy. Sea salt may also taste saltier. This is because supermarket 'free-flowing' salt contains a dilutent, usually magnesium carbonate, which is added to stop the product becoming moist and lumpy.

Sea salt and other brands of so-called 'natural' salt may appeal to you because of their taste, or because of the fun of crunching the coarse grains between your teeth. If you can afford the cost, well and good; but don't buy it believing that it will be especially good for your health.

Juices: Dear But Delicious

Fruit-juices are particularly popular in European countries, especially in Switzerland, where there is widespread belief in their healthgiving properties. In fact, there is very little evidence that the small amounts of minerals, pectin and the like present in these juices do any good of themselves. Some people may benefit from drinking apple juice or prune juice (apart from enjoying their flavour) for the same reason that in the old days overweight squires and fat ladies used to benefit from going to Bath or Baden Baden to 'take the waters': the drinking of fruit-juices or spa waters is commonly associated with *not* eating big meals or with giving up wine.

If you like the taste of prune and apple juice and if you think that they are worth their cost by all means enjoy yourself and drink them. And if by drinking them you can help yourself to keep to a sensible diet on which you don't put on weight, that is better still. But there is no reason to believe that drinking these juices has some unique nutritional virtue: you would probably do as well by drinking a glass of water, which is cheaper. You may say, however – and who am I to argue? – that water is not as tasty.

Dangers in a Vitamin Pill

We all need vitamins in our food, but if we are sensible and eat a reasonable mixture of bread and butter (or margarine which is just as good), potatoes and greens, apples and oranges, meat and fish and all the rest, we get the vitamins we need without buying pills to give us extra vitamins that we *don't* need.

Not only do vitamin pills do sensible eaters no good, there are three ways in which they can do positive harm. Firstly, they cost money and since, of all the deficiencies, a deficiency of money can be most harmful to health, I advise against them. Secondly, those who bother to buy vitamin pills and remember to eat them after meals are the very people who can actually make themselves feel ill by worrying about deficiency diseases they have not got. Finally, by believing in assertions for which there is no evidence, people lay themselves open to the effects of all sorts of wild credulity which, as someone who believes in the use of reason and the importance of having evidence for one's convictions, I regard as being a bad thing, quite apart from any effect it may have on one's health.

VITAMIN C AND COLDS

Vitamin C, also called ascorbic acid, is the vitamin for lack of which the early Arctic explorers and mariners who battled under sail round Cape Horn used to suffer and die from the dreadful disease of scurvy. To protect himself from contracting scurvy a man needs to eat enough potatoes or to drink enough lemon juice to supply himself with about 10 mg of the vitamin every day. Although no one in a civilised country suffers from scurvy nowadays, before potatoes came into general use three centuries or so ago the disease used to be seen quite frequently in the spring and early summer, when green vegetables were difficult to obtain after the long winter. It is usually considered that the amount of vitamin C to satisfy the wants of an ordinary adult with something to spare is between 30 and 70 mg a day.

An American chemist, Linus Pauling, measured how much vitamin C is made in the bodies of rats and dogs and some other animals that make their own vitamin C. The figures he arrived at were large. He then got it into his head that if people ate as much vitamin C as they would have had in their bodies had they not been people at all but rats or dogs, they would not catch cold! He therefore recommended us all to eat anything from 1,000 to 10,000 mg of vitamin C a day – from 30 to 300 times as much as we need to stay well.

Because Pauling is a distinguished chemist, although he never claimed to be an expert on virus diseases such as colds, his idea was seriously considered. No clear evidence, however, has come to light to support his claim that these huge doses of vitamin C have any affect on how often one catches cold or on how severe a cold will be. In fact, the only people who benefit from Pauling's idea are those involved in the manufacture and sale of the vitamin which his faithful followers eat by the teaspoonful.

Popeye's Secret Weapon

However much you may like eating spinach, it is no more nourishing than any other green vegetable: Brussels sprouts, for example, spring greens or turnip tops. But, in the 1930s, when the knowledge of vitamins was in its infancy, it was noted that, just like any other green vegetable, spinach contains vitamin C as well as vitamin A. This knowledge caught the attention of an American cartoonist called Max Fleischer and, just for a joke, he made Popeye the Sailorman eat a can of spinach every time he was getting beaten up in a fight with the result that his strength was miraculously restored. There was just enough truth behind Max Fleischer's joke (namely, that any diet is the better for having greens in it) to establish the idea that spinach has something special about it, and the vegetable thus came to be regarded as something of a wonder food. In fact, too much spinach, particularly if it has been grown on heavily fertilised land, can under certain circumstances be harmful to babies.

That Warm Feeling . . .

An enormous amount of work has been done to find out whether foods grown on land that is fertilised with manure are in any way different in composition from the same foods grown on land which has been treated with so-called 'artificial' fertilisers. Some people take this very seriously, *not* because they can actually point to anybody suffering from eating food grown in this way, but because they feel in their bones that there *must* be something wrong about 'chemical' fertilisers. They also – either consciously or unconsciously – have a warm feeling about manure. (I may say that when a farmer is spreading manure on a field close to a housing estate with the wind in the right quarter, the warm feelings of the house-owners often become noticeably cooler.)

The *facts* are, however, that the composition of the foods we eat, as well as of the hay, silage and turnips that livestock eat, are affected naturally by all sorts of influences: the weather, the kind of soil on which they are grown, the rate of growth of the crop, the total yield, and so forth. All these have a far greater effect on the exact composition and consequent nutritional value of a batch of cabbages or potatoes, wheat or strawberries than whether the fertiliser used to obtain a good harvest is manure or superphosphate out of a bag. In short, so far as it concerns ordinary people, *it does not matter*.

Enthusiasts for 'organic' food also believe that when farmers use insecticides to keep down the greenfly, fungicides to protect their seed from plant diseases or herbicides to kill weeds, traces of these compounds will remain on the food and damage the health of the people eating it. It is obviously prudent for farmers to use these compounds carefully and for there to be appropriate regulations to ensure that our food is not contaminated. And with such careful practice, there is no sound evidence of consumers being injured. Moreover, dear though food has become, it would undoubtedly be dearer still if the growers were not allowed to use these aids to good farming, big yields and high quality. In fact, 'organic' foods *are* more expensive than what can be bought at the super-market and there is no indication that they are in any respect more nourishing.

Of course, excessive use of all kinds of agricultural chemicals is to be avoided, not only because it is wasteful, but also because there is some danger that drinking water may become polluted by contaminated water running off the fields into the rivers, and that the structure of the soil itself may become altered. There are problems for the public-health engineers and the agriculturalists, however; from the nutritionist's point of view, there are no particular advantages to be gained from buying and eating 'organic' food.

'Junk' Foods

People apply this term to all sorts of different foods that they believe to be rubbishy and lacking in nourishment. Unfortunately, those who use this term often speak according to their feelings and beliefs without troubling to consider the facts of the matter, and without taking regard to the whole of the diet of which the 'junk' food is a part. Nor do they always remember that the acceptability of a food is every bit as important as its nutritional value. There was just as much protein in the curate's half-bad egg as in a fresh egg, but no one would willingly eat the half-bad one (except, perhaps, the curate under the eagle eye of his bishop).

In the United States, to take one example, mass-produced hamburgers have been branded as 'junk' foods. Yet their main ingredients are bread (in the form of bun) and minced beef (the hamburger itself), together with onion, tomato and a leaf of lettuce – nutritionally an almost perfect combination. Any justification of the pejorative term 'junk' food, since it cannot refer to nutrition, must therefore be based on the hamburger's being a cheap food popular among working-class people; in fact, on snobbery. I remember in my youth hearing fish and chips (another admirable nutritional mixture) similarly derided by 'superior' critics.

Breakfast cereals are sometimes described as 'junk' foods; indeed I had an uncle, fond of porridge, who, when first told that you could eat cornflakes straight out of the box, asserted that you could do as well if you *ate* the box. The truth is that, while cornflakes and milk are roughly equal in nourishment to bread and milk – but more expensive – most people find the cornflakes pleasanter to eat. They may consider the extra pleasure worth the extra money and they may even *feel* that little bit healthier if they see themselves as part of those unbelievably happy 'cornflakes families' in the television commercials which are paid for by part of that extra money. Of course, eating too much sugar is bad if it leads to obesity. And if people, and particularly children, like the sweet taste of sugar, they may not leave themselves appetite enough to eat all the other foods they need. The sensible mother may, however, consider breakfast cereals worth the money if, because the children like them, they come down to breakfast in good time and willingly drink the milk poured on to the cereal.

Don't be fooled, however, if the breakfast cereal manufacturers make great play of the fact that their products contain added pyridoxine or riboflavine or vitamin this or that. All these may be listed on the packet and the impression is put about that the breakfast cereal in question – made from sun-tanned wheat, or sun-soaked rice, or even sun-drenched corn – is peculiarly beneficial to children. Most of this is nonsense. There is no reason to doubt that the children who eat these cereals are obtaining as much of these vitamins as they need anyway. At best it can be said that no harm is likely to come to them if they eat more of half a dozen vitamins than they need. At worst, the product is made unnecessarily dear; besides which, nobody wants to be told that a breakfast cereal is *extra good* when, in fact, it is merely *just as good as, but no better than,* any other.

Chocolate bars and candy bars in all their elaborate variety may also be categorised as 'junk' foods. Undoubtedly, their main attraction and the principal justification for their existence is the possibility they offer for self-indulgence in a sweet and attractive taste and in a consistency and appearance calculated to please. Because they are usually eaten at odd times between meals, and because of their appealing taste and softness they are a temptation to overeating and the dangers of that all-too-common dietary disease, obesity. Like breakfast cereals, they may so blunt the keenness of a child's appetite that he may fail to eat the less immediately attractive foods he needs, like vegetables; to that extent, therefore, candy can justifiably be described as 'junk'. On the other hand, chocolate bars and the like often contain dried milk, sometimes butter and always the energy-value which active children – whatever reproving parents may think – do need from the sweetmeats they clamour for.

Those who attack so-called 'junk' foods sometimes do so in the belief that they do harm to the nutrition of those who eat them. But a more valid accusation would be that the cost per unit of nourishment of a fancy breakfast cereal or candy bar is higher than the equivalent food value to be obtained from simple staple foods. The problem is, however, that people are very often prepared to pay for what they like, even when money is scarce. This is why they will, if they can afford to do so, pay much more for steak than for mince or corned beef in spite of knowing that they are paying only for a delicious flavour and texture, not for extra nourishment. In fact, when ordinary folk spend money on jellies and 'whips' and their richer neighbours treat themselves to sorbets, these – 'junk' foods indeed – are alike amusement and pleasure combined with virtually no nourishment at all.

Better Cooked

'Some cakes . . . are little less than an exercise
in self-indulgence, and some children can only be
described as greedy.'

AT ONE TIME some people used to try to persuade their fellow citizens that cooking was a *bad thing* and that the nutritional value of our food would be improved if we all ate it raw. Although there are still a few of these enthusiasts about, it is now generally recognised that the effects of cooking can be a mixture of good and bad. Most of them are desirable and contribute substantially to good nutrition.

Why Cook?

DIGESTIBILITY

Bread – the staff of life and the basis of every sandwich – biscuits, cakes and pastries are all made from wheat flour. Flour, however, is virtually inedible unless it is cooked. Starch, which is the main ingredient of flour, occurs in the form of little granules, which in chemical terms are rather like tightly rolled-up balls of wool that can only be unravelled slowly and incompletely by the digestive juices. The heat of the oven during baking splits open these granules, so that the digestive mechanism then has no difficulty in dealing with them.

Rice, barley and other grains are similar to wheat. Everybody knows that uncooked rice is quite uneatable, so it obviously cannot contribute to nutrition. The heat of cooking gradually disentangles the starch granules, so that one can eat, digest and benefit from rice pudding.

Potatoes have protein in them and vitamin C as well, together with small amounts of other useful substances, but the main component (next to water) is starch, which is why chunks of uncooked potato are barely eatable. On the other hand, once the structure of the potato has been disrupted and softened by the heat of boiling water, or of hot frying fat or of the oven, its nutritional content becomes available to the eater.

Just as raw flour, barley and oatmeal are uneatable, hard structures such as dried peas and beans are too tough and strong to be chewed up, far less digested. To convert dried peas and beans into eatable food, they must first be soaked to allow water to penetrate into their cells. Then, when they are boiled or baked, the heat brings about a formation and expansion of steam that together break down the foundation structure to leave us with a useful, nourishing food that can be broken down further still by the digestive juices in the gut and converted into a kind of 'soup' which soaks through the gut wall into the bloodstream.

The effect of cooking on animal foods is rather different. Raw meat is perfectly digestible, although it can be tough. Though it is not hard like raw potato, it may be difficult to chew, and the same goes for fish and poultry as well. Most meat is made up of the muscles of animals or birds, and muscle is composed of strong, elastic fibres. When a cook beats a steak with a mallet the bundles of muscle fibres are broken apart: this makes the meat muscle weaker or, in more familiar terms, it 'tenderises' the steak. The heat of cooking shrinks the fibres, disrupting the original strength and integrity of the muscular tissue and softening its structure still further.

SAFETY

Pigs occasionally suffer from an infection called *trichinosis*. The microscopic parasites can gain access to your body if you eat infected meat, and if they do so you will contract a long and serious illness from which, indeed, you may never fully recover. Cooking destroys the infection and makes the meat safe. It is therefore very important – far more so that the loss of a few per cent of this or that vitamin – to make sure that bacon, ham, pork and even sausages are properly cooked before they are eaten.

Trichinosis, though comparatively rare, is important because it is so dangerous and persistent a disease. But animals and birds can also suffer from other diseases, including *salmonellosis*, which is infection by one or other of the bacteria that cause food poisoning. Most people are tough enough to be able to put up with a few of these bacteria, but if they eat too many of them in their food they may well suffer for it. It is thus good sense to cook all sorts of meat thoroughly, including chicken and other kinds of poultry and game, so as to kill any bacteria infecting it – quite apart from the fact that most of us prefer the taste of our meat and poultry cooked.

COOKING IMPROVES FLAVOUR

'Health' enthusiasts sometimes forget that no matter how many vitamins some food item may contain, it will not do anyone any good if it is so nasty – or so tough – that nobody will eat it. This is another mistake made by the raw-vegetable brigade: while raw cabbage, for instance, does contain more vitamin C than cooked cabbage does, the difference is effectively cancelled out upon the plate, because a helping of cooked cabbage contains much more cabbage than a raw serving does.

For most of us, good cooking contributes hugely to the enjoyment of our meals – consider only the crisp crackling of roast pork, the crust on home-made bread, the soft, fluffy interior of a perfectly baked potato, or whatever your particular favourites may be. Because the smell, taste, appearance and texture of well-cooked food are attractive, people are encouraged to eat more. If they were eating too little before, this is *good*. If they were eating all they needed before, and more, this is *bad* because they may become fat.

Damage a Bad Cook Can Do

A great deal of scientists' time has been devoted to

investigating what happens to the protein, the vitamins and the minerals when different foods are cooked in different ways. If you burn the toast to a cinder, naturally you destroy its nutritional value. Where a cooking process demands a *very* hot oven – for example, in the baking of water biscuits – there is less vitamin in the product than in the starting material. In general, however, *well-cooked food is nourishing food*. And the opposite can be equally true. When cabbage is 'boiled to rags', most of its nourishment is knocked out of it. In particular, food that has been kept hot for a long time loses not only its good flavour but some of its nutritional virtues as well.

HOT FOOD AND COLD

The temperature of food has virtually no effect on its nutritional value, though a dish which is delicious when it is piping hot may be disgusting when it is tepid and worse when it is stone cold. But this example of bad cooking at least has no influence on its nourishment, unless the cold food is so unappetising that it is not eaten at all.

FRESH FOOD AND STALE

Obviously, if food that has 'gone off' has been infected with bacteria that cause illness, it will be harmful to eat it. For the most part, however, the bacteria that cause food to decay do not affect people's health. Not everybody enjoys the taste of sour milk or stale eggs, but nutritionally they are as good as ever. Indeed, game used at one time to be praised when it was 'high', which is only a polite way of saying that it was partly putrefied. One reason why curry is popular in tropical climates is because its strongly tasting spices mask the aroma of decay which can develop all too quickly in meat in hot weather. On the other hand, vegetables have lost some of their nutritional value once their crisp freshness has disappeared and they have begun to wilt.

Mixing Things Up

One great advantage of cooking is that it makes it easy to follow the principle which, of all others, underlies good nutrition: to eat a wide variety of all the different foodstuffs. Cooking is the ideal way to achieve the rich and complex mixtures upon which good nutrition is based.

Take a glance at a cookery book to settle the point, starting with soup, whether something as esoteric as borsch or as commonplace as Scotch broth. We find in these recipes excellent combinations of ingredients, nicely compounded to contribute to a balanced diet. (Indeed, traditional dishes, once jeered at by food snobs and even now censured by 'health food' devotees, are more often than not an education in good nutrition and sensible eating.) *Borsch*, for instance, is based on bone stock simmered with pork, so that animal protein will complement the protein of the vegetable ingredients – beetroots, carrots and celery – and a garnish of parsley and cream adds calories and vitamins as well.

The Russian countryfolk who invented borsch may not have been professional nutritional scientists any more than were the Scots who invented *Scotch broth*. This combines mutton, which again provides animal protein, with carrots, turnips, leeks and parsley, and finally pearl barley to supply 'body' – what the scientist might call calories.

Perhaps only today, when costs are rising and we therefore value what we buy, do we fully appreciate how excellent is the British combination of *fish and chips*. Piled up together in a steaming tasty plateful, the fish protein supplements the vegetable protein of the flour in the batter and of the potatoes, which also contribute vitamin C. The egg in the batter provides some iron and vitamin A, with the starch of the batter and the potatoes contributing to the energy-value of the whole.

Roast beef, Yorkshire pudding and 'two veg', at one time the regular Sunday dinner of the British, is another mixture that is both delightful to eat and close to nutritional perfection, the animal protein of the beef rounding off the vegetable protein of the pudding, with the minerals and vitamins of the cabbage and potato supplementing the whole. Look, too, at recipes for *shepherd's pie* and *Cornish pasties* – two other traditional dishes that admirably combine meat protein and vegetable protein with essential energy-value, and which when really well made are quite delicious.

And I must include here a word in favour of *cake*. Linked to this, I consider that it is also seemly to write a sentence or two in favour of children. In both instances, it is important to discriminate. Some cakes (particularly if they are called by the French term, *gâteau*) are little less than an exercise in self-indulgence, and some children can only be described as greedy. Honest-to-God cake, however, can make an excellent contribution to good nutrition, and there are very many children whose instincts for healthy eating are sounder than the more informed convictions of their elders.

It is true that *Dundee cake* contains sugar, as well as flour and butter. To my mind, much of the objection to this sugar is not that it is likely to hurt the children who eat it but that – being agreeable to taste – it may somehow be bad for their characters. Anyway, the recipe then calls for eggs which add all sorts of good nutritional things, dried fruit which supplies iron, and almonds which provide still more protein. Most kinds of cake consist basically of flour, butter, sugar and eggs, and clearly such mixtures constitute a virtual meal in themselves. While a husband can legitimately scold his wife for neglecting her diet if for breakfast she only has bread and butter and a cup of tea, he can smile approval if she has a boiled egg as well. A truly scientific husband would be equally happy if, looking back as he went off to work, he saw his wife eating a slice of cake. Marie Antoinette was said to have suggested that the poor, unable to buy bread, should eat cake; she may have been weak on politics but she obviously had a grasp of the principles of nutrition.

Puddings, too, commonly neglected by nutritionists, demonstrate equally well the benefits of cooking. Slices of bread and butter left over from tea-time and going stale, are likely to remain uneaten and nutritionally useless; but add some currants and candied peel, an egg, milk and sugar and the mixture, in the hands of a good cook, becomes something memorable as *bread-and-butter pudding*. Even the humble *rice pudding* has virtue in the way that the nutritional value of rice is enhanced by baking it with milk.

For people who easily put on weight, and who are therefore well aware that they tend to consume too much energy-value, *jam roly-poly*, made from flour, suet and jam, is obviously not an appropriate mixture. But how could any academic thinker improve on the subtle virtues of *Eve's pudding* in which the cook compounds apples and lemon rind together with flour, sugar and butter, and an egg? Bravo!

'Kissing Don't Last: Cookery Do'

As well as putting together meals that are good mixtures of all the different nutrients and that are digestible and safe to eat, the good cook has another very important role. For it is upon the cook that, in the end, the quality of the meal depends: and whether or not a dish is actually eaten may well depend on whether it is attractively presented and whether it tastes good. The imaginative cook takes trouble to select foods that complement each other in flavour, seasons them temptingly, perhaps using herbs or spices to give variety and piquancy, and then combines them into appetising menus. He – or she – chooses foods that contrast enjoyably in texture (as crisp pastry complements the soft juicy fruit in an apple pie, or crunchy croutons add interest to a smooth creamy soup), in colour (why else do we garnish an omelette with vivid green parsley, or put scarlet cherries on top of a trifle?) and sometimes even in temperature as well, as when hot chocolate sauce is poured over ice cream.

But all this trouble is well repaid by the pleasure that a delicious meal gives to those who eat it: good cooking is certainly one of the most agreeable ways of putting love into nutrition.

SIX

Pets

'Konrad Lorenz tells the story of his redoubtable cockatoo,
which was unable to resist the appeal of buttons . . .'

THIS BOOK is aimed at describing how you and your family can be well fed, and I do not intend to leave out those members of the family who are sometimes over-looked: the dogs and cats, and even the budgerigars, tortoises and pet snakes – after all, about half of all the households in Great Britain include a pet.

Broadly speaking, the nutritional needs of animals are roughly the same as ours. This, of course, is why scientists can use rats and mice, guinea pigs and even sometimes pigeons and chickens to study the nutrition of people. The feeding of animals also shows very directly how the amounts of this or that vitamin, of protein, fat and all the other food constituents are only part of the story. One of the other parts, which can be every bit as important, is that animals – like people – will go to great lengths to eat the foods that they like. The same principle applies to koala bears, which are much commoner than giant pandas and much easier to breed. In fact, there is outside Brisbane a prosperous little private park which makes a good living from breeding and selling cuddly koala bears as pets, and also from supplying the customers with deep-frozen packets of the eucalyptus leaves the koalas like to eat.

The different kinds of animals that live on the earth *are* different because each has evolved so as to suit the special circumstances existing in its own particular habitat. Polar bears fit into the Arctic scene because they are born with thick white fur and so can survive where warm fur coats are an advantage, and also because they flourish on a diet of fish and seals. Penguins, too, do well in the snow and ice of the Antarctic because they have a special supply of blood to keep their feet warm, and it is on their warm feet that they balance their eggs which otherwise would never hatch out in the bitter cold. These are highly specialised animals which for that reason (and for others as well) are seldom kept as pets. Animals can be divided into three broad groups according to the main kinds of food they eat. There are the herbivorous creatures that live largely on vegetables and plants; the carnivorous animals that live largely on flesh; and the omnivorous animals that – more adaptable than the others – live on anything. We ourselves are the best examples of omnivorous animals, which is the reason why human beings are to be found everywhere on the globe eating meat and vegetables indiscriminately. The Australian Aborigines eat insects, Africans eat the roots of the manioc plant, for centuries the Chinese used to eat dogs, and the Scots eat haggis.

But even though animals can be categorised according to the kind of food they eat, some of them show a measure of tolerance in their selection of food, and these in the main are the animals that are kept as pets. It is a nuisance, to say the least, to keep a pet that will eat only bamboo shoots or the leaves of a particular eucalyptus tree. One reason why dogs and cats have been so readily accepted as pets is that although they are primarily carnivorous, they can also get along on a mixture of animal and vegetable foods.

All animals, even the most tolerant – such as goats and ostriches, which have a reputation for eating almost anything – retain their own particular likes and dislikes. Nevertheless the actual average biochemical requirements, expressed in terms of vitamins, protein, minerals, fat and calories, can be listed for animal species just as they can for people, and all this is especially valuable to the manufacturers of pet foods which, like our own 'convenience foods', are selling in increasing quantities. I am not altogether sure, however, whether it serves any useful purpose to insist, as do the control authorities in the United States, that pet-food manufacturers should ensure that their products contain minimum quantities of a whole list of nutrients as laid down by the experts of the United States National Academy of Science. Clearly, this only has practical importance where the pet animal lives wholly or mainly on a single manufactured product. After all, animals – again, like people – don't choose to ingest vitamins, minerals and all the rest; they just eat food.

The Well-fed Dog

Nutritionally speaking at least, dogs are remarkably like people, except that they are smaller and consequently need less to eat, and that their life-span is shorter so that they pass from puppyhood to adulthood and thence to old age more quickly. Nor do dogs require vitamin C in their diet, so they do not need orange juice or fresh fruit, potatoes or greens every day in their diet as we do.

To feed a puppy properly is thus rather like feeding a child. A puppy is small, active and growing; because it has a small stomach – just as a small child has – it should be fed frequently, say four times a day. It may be given milk with sugar, brown bread and perhaps cereal for breakfast and much the same again at midday, with a main meal of finely chopped meat in the late afternoon, and sweetened milk again at bedtime, with perhaps a hard biscuit to amuse it before it goes to sleep. As the puppy grows, it will eat bigger meals and the number can gradually be reduced to two a day by the time it is a year old. At the same time the milk mixture can be cut down and the meat meal increased. The growing puppy needs milk to supply calcium for its bones and teeth, and reputable dog foods, both dry and moist, have calcium added to them. Dogs like bones partly because they find them fun to struggle with and partly because, even though they do not actually eat very much of them, they eat enough to contribute to their intake of calcium.

Dogs like meat, but they can thrive quite well on an appropriate mixture of vegetable foods. Indeed, many proprietary pet foods contain 'artificial meat' made out of texturised soya-bean protein. And before the modern 'semi-moist' products were invented, dogs did quite well on a mixture of meat and dog biscuits.

Now that the availability of a huge range of pet foods (most of which are almost as nourishing as the advertisements claim) makes it easy to feed the fussiest of dogs, malnutrition is unlikely, provided the owner is prepared to spend the necessary money. But with dogs, again as with people, the commonest form of malnutrition is obesity. It has been estimated that something like one dog in three is markedly overweight, and when mild obesity is taken into account the proportion is much higher.

Dogs, like their masters, do better if they do not eat between meals. Furthermore, the amount of food they are given should be adjusted to their size, the amount of exercise they take and whether or not they are overweight. The overfed, overweight, under-exercised lap-dog, over-indulged by a loving but ill-judging mistress, is a horrible warning to dogs and owners alike. Fat dogs (and other animals too) are especially subject to disease, particularly to arthritis and to skin and respiratory disorders.

Nevertheless most owners of fat dogs get tremendous pleasure from feeding their animals, and it may be very hard to recognise that in order to help Rover back to normal health and weight you must deny yourself the pleasure of satisfying the yearning in those melting brown eyes by slipping your pet a chocolate or a fragment of cake. The most useful response to a dog's persistent begging for titbits is probably to take him for a walk: this removes him from temptation and provides him with some healthy exercise. The owner is likely to benefit from the exercise too: many of those whose dogs are too fat are themselves under-exercised and overfed.

Dogs can, if not properly fed, suffer from some of the same deficiency diseases as people. Puppies which are not given milk, particularly if they are at the same time given too much bread, biscuit, sugar and the like, may develop rickets, and a spoonful of cod-liver oil now and then ensures their protection. It could also be usefully given to a bitch while she is carrying her litter.

Since dogs' diets are usually less varied than ours it is wise to give them brown bread rather than white, and it is also sensible to take some care over cooking their meat. It is best for a puppy – and the dog it is going to grow into – to have its meat cooked in order to ensure that it is not infected with food-poisoning organisms. This protects the puppy and also the children (and you) who play with it and – for all I know – kiss its little nose. Even though the dog meat you buy may not be up to the culinary standard you would choose for yourself, you should cook it to about the same degree as you would cook meat for the family. If you boil it 'to rags' you will reduce its vitamin content.

Feeding Felines

The nutritional needs of a cat are broadly similar to a dog's: that is, they are much like our own except that it does not need vitamin C. The main reason why cat owners, given half a chance, talk at length about their cats' diets and why the manufacturers so often bring out new and fancy cat-food mixtures is not because cats are, in nutritional terms, at all difficult to nourish. It is because cats are discriminating animals which – like the temperamental actors and actresses they are – develop their own likes and dislikes. These likes may be only indirectly concerned with nutrition, however, as when the cat brings a dead bird or a decapitated mouse indoors just to show you how clever it is.

Kittens, like puppies – or human babies – do best on a diet based on milk. Like puppies, their stomachs are small and they can only consume the amount of food they require in a series of small feeds. The best way to raise a well-nourished kitten is to arrange for the services of an intelligent cat to look after it.

Grown-up cats do best on two meals a day: a light meal in the morning and their main meal in the evening. Once again, the basic rules of nutrition apply. First, give your cat enough to eat but not too much. This is usually no problem because cats, being strikingly clever and independent animals which do not wait to be taken for walks but organise their own exercise, usually have too much sense to allow themselves to get fat. Lazy cats, especially neutered toms, may however have to have their food restricted.

Cats, being carnivores, like meat. In nutritional terms, fish is broadly similar to meat. Whether you give meat or fish to your cat is largely a matter of taste (either yours or the cat's). Given the chance, however, cats will also eat a pretty wide variety of foods, which is the second principle of good nutrition. Although they will not hesitate to tell you – in no uncertain terms – what their likes and dislikes are, they are also sufficiently bright, when the chips are down, to eat what is available even if they do not particularly like it rather than starve themselves – though an enterprising cat will often seek more palatable food elsewhere, or hunt it for itself. Many cats eat at two homes, as well as catching mice and birds. All the same, the prudent cat-owner will make provision for his pet to enjoy some variety in its food: besides meat, fish, tripe and the like, it can also be given bread and other cereal foods as well as, of course, milk. In fact, if *you* are eating a sensible diet, it – or what remains of it after you have done – will nourish your cat too.

Alternatively, the proprietary cat-foods, if you are prepared to spend the money on them, are nourishing, convenient and have been specially compounded to appeal to the palates of the most discriminating and fussy cats. But you should remember that they are designed to be complete foods, and do not need any supplementing with extra snacks and titbits.

Cats are often sensible to be fussy if, by being so, they can avoid giving themselves food poisoning. You can help them by serving their meat and fish cooked rather than raw, and by keeping their feeding utensils clean.

Rabbits are Easy

Though its nutritional needs are much like those of a dog or cat, the diet of a rabbit is quite different because, unlike those two, a rabbit is basically a vegetarian.

Rabbits are easy to feed. To start with, you will have little of the trouble that feeding puppies and kittens can give, because the doe will look after the baby rabbits for you. Her success in doing this is one reason why rabbits multiply as vigorously as they proverbially do. Indeed, rabbits throughout their lives show their powers of survival and multiplication by taking their existence (and their food) as it comes with none of the fussiness exhibited by some cats – and, come to that, some people.

Pet rabbits do quite well on two meals a day but, unlike cats and dogs, they actually benefit from having something to nibble between meals. In the morning, a stiff mash of, say, bread, breakfast cereal, bran or porridge, cooked greens and boiled potatoes and sometimes a little milk will set them off to a good start. The evening meal can then comprise cabbage leaves, raw carrot, fresh grass or other herbage or, when fresh leaves are unavailable, hay. It is because leaves and grass contain so large a proportion of water that a rabbit needs to spend so much of its time eating. Even so, a pet rabbit must always be provided with fresh drinking water.

As a herbivore, a rabbit eats a comparatively restricted diet, without meat or fish, eggs or cheese. To make up for this, it has evolved an ingenious trick, namely to eat some of its own droppings, thus making use of vitamins produced by the micro-organisms which live in its intestines. One of these vitamins in particular is mainly provided in our own diet by the meat we eat. The pellets may also contribute to the protein quality of the diet. It is important not to prevent the rabbit from indulging in this rather unusual habit, as otherwise it could suffer from nutritional deficiency.

Though rabbits are easy to feed, there are one or two precautions to take. Never feed your rabbit *raw* potato and particularly raw potatoes that have gone green in the sun: these contain enough poisonous solanine to kill it. Similarly, never feed it rhubarb leaves: the oxalate in them is poisonous. Do not feed it solely on cabbage: there may be sufficient goitre-producing material in them to give the rabbit goitre. Don't give your rabbit yew, buttercups, foxgloves, laurel, privet, laburnum or the leaves of daffodils, narcissi or hyacinths: they are all, to a degree, poisonous. And never feed it deadly nightshade; it might come to no harm if you did, but should you decide to strike the animal off your list of pets and eat it, its flesh would poison *you*.

Guinea Pigs are Like People

A guinea pig, like a rabbit, is a vegetarian. But although it likes to eat very much the same kinds of food that rabbits do, its nutritional needs are quite similar to our own. Guinea pigs, like people but unlike dogs and cats, need vitamin C. In fact, it was from feeding guinea pigs unsatisfactory human diets lacking in fruit and vegetables that basic knowledge about vitamin C first came to light.

Guinea pigs are bright little creatures. They like to nibble at their food throughout the day. On the other hand, they can thrive on two meals a day plus extras, much as rabbits do, so they can be fed the same stiff mixture of bread, cereals, greens and potatoes followed by an evening meal of greenstuff. Or they can be given a mixture of bran and grain as compounded for chickens and pigs, together with plenty of fresh greenstuff – some ingenious people keep their guinea pigs in cages without bottoms which they move day by day across the lawn, thus getting their pets to cut the grass.

Guinea pigs, like rabbits, are very little trouble to raise largely because their young are born so well developed that their 'puppydom' presents few problems. They run about as soon as they are born and though for the first few days they enjoy a little bread and milk it is not long before they settle down to nibble with the rest of the family.

Mice Need More Than Cheese

Rats are second only to man in dietetic virtuosity. They eat practically anything: this is one reason why they are found almost everywhere on the earth. So feeding rats, whether it is pet white rats from choice or wild grey rats because you cannot avoid them, or feeding white mice or the intrusive house variety, is very much like feeding people. Except that rats and mice do not need vitamin C, they need all the same nutrients that we do. They are also good house-keepers so that it does not matter whether you give them set meals or – which is more sensible – provide them with food and water and let them organise their own lives.

Pet rats and mice need variety, like the rest of us. They will do very well on chicken feed, or on a mixture of grain of various sorts together with peas and beans. Wild mice like cheese, though they do not live entirely on it any more than we do. If you find that cheese makes your pet mouse's cage smelly, a little baby-food, which is mainly dried milk, is just as good. Meat can be awkward to feed to pet rats and mice and you must make sure that it does not go bad; alternatively, the made-up mixtures sold in pet shops often contain meat meal. Rolled oats or other breakfast cereal with a little bird-seed can be used as the basis for a good mixture. The food should be lightly salted just as a good cook salts food for the table, and if you have young pet rats and mice, then cod-liver oil in the mixture will protect them against rickets. An occasional feed of fresh greenstuff is useful, not because the animals need vitamin C but for its other ingredients, and a piece of carrot helps to diversify the mixture further.

Keeping Hamsters Happy ...

A hamster is a cheerful robust little creature which, like the rats and mice that are its near relations, is not at all fussy about what it eats or when it eats it. Hamsters, however, must have sufficient housing to allow each animal to have a 'room' to itself. When they are together they tend to quarrel and, as everyone knows, quarrelling tends to take away one's appetite. Even to get them to mate is quite difficult because the females are usually more militant than the males and bully their husbands.

Their other peculiarity is that they are terrible misers. If you give them more than they can eat, they stuff what they don't need into their cheek pouches and then carry it away to store it in a corner where it may go stale and smell.

Hamsters eat almost anything. Dog biscuits, bread, wheat, oats, barley, cornflakes, carrots, any kinds of greens, hay – plenty of hay is a good idea, partly for food and partly for bedding – apples, turnips, a little milk mixed in occasionally, egg, worms, caterpillars, bacon rind, raisins, nuts. In fact, the only foods that do not agree with them very well are chocolate, oranges, grapefruit and lemons. All you need to do, therefore, is just to apply the rules of nutrition: give them enough to eat but not too much, and vary the mixture from time to time.

... and Gerbils Jumping

A gerbil is another jolly little jumping creature which has been carried away from the arid deserts of Asia and Africa to the luxurious accommodation provided for the pets of western children. Like hamsters, they are quite closely related to the rat tribe, and like them too, are not especially particular about their food. The pet-food people market a packeted feed for gerbils which is in small lumps, convenient for the creatures to nibble at. Or you can give them the sorts of things I suggested for hamsters. In short, if you supply them with good variety, they will look after themselves – after all, rats do, don't they?

Gerbils are nocturnal animals when they are in the wild. It should, therefore, be no surprise if they sleep during the day and take their meals and get their exercise at night. Their food should, therefore, be available to them then. Of course, contact with people may give them the idea of enjoying – as some of us do – 'night life', which for them means staying up in the daytime.

Dormice are Demanding

A dormouse is not a mouse at all but belongs to a different species altogether. It is a hibernating animal and although it will not sleep the whole winter if you keep it indoors in the warm, it does better if it is kept outside and allowed to sleep from autumn until spring. When it wakes up it is very hungry and, although like other animals it obeys the general rules of nutrition, its likes and dislikes are so pronounced that it is almost essential to give it what it likes, based on its habits in the wild, if you want it to thrive. It will therefore need grain of various sorts (wheat, oats, barley, rice or maize), nuts, seeds, berries and sliced fruit. Perhaps one of the reasons why dormice are not particularly popular pets is because they like to eat 'meat' in the form of mealworms and grubs. Indeed, they are fond of all sorts of insects. It is particularly important, however, to remember to ensure that pet dormice have plenty of fresh water to drink.

Two notes on teeth

☐ Dormice, like most other rodents – and these include rabbits, guinea pigs, hamsters, gerbils, rats and mice – need to keep their teeth in order by gnawing, and they often gnaw the woodwork of their cages. But if they do not live in wooden cages or if you don't want them to gnaw their way to freedom, you should make sure that they have a fairly regular ration of hard food to gnaw upon.

☐ Dormice have projecting front teeth. If you decide to keep them as pets, therefore, remember that although they are in general docile animals, they can give you a very nasty bite.

Birds in Fine Feather

Some birds, like some animals, eat almost anything: vegetables, fruit, seeds or meat. There are others – birds of prey, for example, which are not often kept as pets – that live on little else than meat. And there are vegetarian birds, though of course it is no use providing a bird with a soft beak designed for eating soft fruit and insects with nuts so hard that it is unable to get at the kernels inside. But regardless of the menu they fancy, birds have much the same nutritional requirements as our own. There are, of course, some differences. A laying hen needs proportionately more calcium than we do in order to build up the shells of her eggs, and few birds (with the exception of the red-vented bulbul) need any vitamin C at all. In general, however, the rules of nutrition that apply to us apply to them.

And birds can suffer from our own deficiency diseases. Researchers used pigeons and chickens to study vitamin B_1 deficiency, and young chicks to investigate the way vitamin D protects them, much as it protects young children, against rickets.

CANARIES

Canaries could be described as the 'sparrows' of Madeira and the Canary Isles, where they fly about wild and pick up a living without too much trouble just as sparrows do in cooler climates. Pet canaries are usually given a ready-prepared seed mixture, together with a little fresh green food such as grass, rape, lettuce, watercress, dandelion leaves or chickweed. An occasional piece of sponge cake or the yolk of a hard-boiled egg, plus grated apple or carrot ensure that all the varied nutrients are provided. Like all cage birds, canaries must always have fresh drinking water available to them.

BUDGERIGARS

Budgerigars are small parakeets which originally came from Australia where flocks of them fly around the saltbush flats, living mainly on grass-seed. When kept as pets, they do quite well on much the same mixture as that given to canaries, that is to say on packeted bird-seed diversified with, say, a spray of millet, a few tufts of grass that has gone to seed, together with greenstuff and fruit.

Cage birds can make use of a piece of cuttle fish or some similar hard thing to peck at in order to keep their beaks filed down. A block of iodised salt serves the same purpose and also supplies the bird with salt as it wants it. Birds also need grit from which they can select and swallow pieces of an appropriate size so that when their food reaches their crops it is rolled around with the gritty stones and thus ground up till it is reduced to mush. This system serves the same purpose as teeth, which birds do not possess.

PARROTS

Parrots are less popular as pets than they once were, now that houses tend to be smaller and people fuss more about tidiness and polish than they did in the past. Parrots undoubtedly do scatter their food about and make a mess. They are also big and sometimes noisy birds; moreover, imported birds can infect their owners with an unpleasant illness.

So far as feeding goes, the well-fed parrot needs very much the same as the well-fed budgerigar, except that everything will be on a larger scale: for instance, the seeds in the mixed-seed combination can be bigger. Sunflower or pumpkin seeds, for example, are big enough to allow the bird to pick them up in its claws to eat. Konrad Lorenz tells the story of his redoubtable cockatoo, which was unable to resist the appeal of buttons – presumably confusing them with seeds or beans. Not content with regularly biting them off the weekly washing as it hung up to dry in the garden, he once approached a harmless elderly guest as he slumbered peacefully in the sunshine, and delicately removed every single button from his clothes – jacket, waistcoat and trousers as well!

A daily ration of fruit and leaves should be provided as well as the seed mixture. Parrots are also fond of nuts and, as a treat, will enjoy a piece of cake or a biscuit.

INDIAN MINA BIRD

This is a shining black bird about the size of a smallish crow. It is popular because it is probably the bird which can best be taught to imitate human speech; but it is noisy, messy, and rather faddy about its food. A compounded poultry meal is a convenient basic ration, but the mina likes fruit as well and does best when it has some live mealworms every day.

Tortoises, Turtles, Terrapins

These creatures, which are all related, belong to one of the most ancient families of reptiles in the world. There were tortoises before the dinosaurs appeared, and – who knows? – they may outlive mankind. One reason for their survival is that they are not very active and consequently do not need very much to eat. Pet tortoises need feeding only two or three times a week and can go for days quite happily without food at all.

LAND TORTOISES

These are the animals most commonly kept as pets, and they are usually vegetarians, although there are exceptions: the box turtle, for instance, starts life as a meat-eater and becomes a vegetarian only in its later years. Pet tortoises eat lettuce, cabbage and greens of all sorts, peas and pea pods, shredded carrots and tomatoes, bananas and apples. If you keep them in your garden, they will unerringly develop a taste for your favourite flowers. They will also eat bread, and should always be provided with water. Because they are slow feeders, they must be given time to plough through their meals, but don't leave their food lying around so long that it goes bad.

WATER TORTOISES

These animals (also called turtles or terrapins) are dangerous – not because they might bite you, but because they are very likely to give food poisoning to those who look after them, partly because they are liable to contract food poisoning themselves and partly because they foul the water as they swim about their tank or pond so that it can become very seriously contaminated. If then the boys and girls who care for them pick them up to see how they are getting on and then (without washing their hands) sit down to dinner, food poisoning may start up in the family. In the United States, only water tortoises hatched from eggs certified as being salmonella-free may legally be sold. Even this, however, is not a sure protection. One reason is that water tortoises like meat and enjoy chopped beef, offal, fish – in fact, they thrive on canned dog-food. There is always a chance that water tortoises' meat is itself contaminated and that – slow eaters as they are – the contamination grows worse as time passes. And the risks are increased further because water tortoises like to have their food actually dropped into the water in which they are swimming. Even though this makes it easier for them to get at it, it will go bad more readily and particularly if there are scraps of it (as there surely will be) that the animals do not eat straight away.

If, after all this, you *really* want to keep water tortoises, however, you can minimise the dangers of food poisoning by frequently and conscientiously cleaning out their tanks, and by scrupulously washing your hands after handling them – and seeing that the rest of the family does the same. You can feed your somewhat insalubrious pets on vegetables, fruit and meat with occasional servings of bread or other cereal food. Many water tortoises enjoy live 'meat', such as crickets or earthworms. If yours do, their taste should be gratified wherever possible. They do need quite a lot of calcium in their food, because of their need to grow a shell, and it is a good idea, therefore, to sprinkle their food occasionally with bone meal.

Three Thousand Lizards

Tortoises and turtles are old, but lizards are older still and date back to remote antiquity. They are 'cold-blooded' creatures – meaning that their blood is at the same temperature as the environment in which they live (which is usually hot) – so that, not having to find the energy to heat themselves up and spending most of their time standing still, they do not need much food. However, since they have been on earth a long time, they have come to expect the food they *do* consume to be just how they like it.

There are about 3,000 different kinds of lizard and what you need to give your lizard to eat depends on the kind you have chosen to keep as a pet. Most of them are carnivorous and you may need to provide them, say, three times a week with live earthworms and crickets. Others like spiders and flies as well. Mealworms are also popular and may be easier to obtain. Lizards need water but the smaller ones, not being accustomed to drinking from a bowl, can best obtain what they need from droplets provided for them by your sprinkling water over their living area.

In the United States, where things are often bigger than they are elsewhere, some people keep iguana lizards as pets. These creatures, if properly fed, may grow 6 ft long! They can be fed on lettuce, kale, fruit and an occasional serving of dog-food, together with a sprinkling of bone meal and a teaspoonful of cod-liver oil now and again. Although they can manage on three feeds a week, they grow more quickly when they are fed every day.

Simple Rules for Snakes

The snakes are related to the lizards; they also are 'cold-blooded', inactive animals, and consequently do not need much to eat. Small snakes need feeding only once or twice a week, and bigger snakes manage quite well on a meal once a month or so. Their digestive mechanism is undemanding, too, and snakes, far from producing their droppings regularly each day, may only excrete them once or twice a month – which makes pet snakes popular with their owners. Snakes shed their skins periodically; immediately after doing this they tend to be hungry and need feeding. Snakes need water not only to drink but also to bath in.

Snakes are carnivorous, and their likes and dislikes are clear and definite. They prefer to eat their 'meat' alive. This is sensible, because by eating the whole animal, including its internal organs – and by eating it quite fresh at that – they are virtually certain to obtain all their nutritional needs. The civilised grass snakes of Great Britain can be persuaded to eat freshly killed frogs, worms and various kinds of insect. Larger snakes usually thrive best on a diet of white mice, white rats, chicks, hamsters (if the snake-lovers can bear to put them on the menu) as well as frogs and other reptiles. But remember that even if your pet snake *is* prepared to eat its food dead, you still have the problem of getting hold of the various items in the first place. And if you do feed, say, a live rat to your snake, make sure that the snake eats the rat within a reasonable period of time or you may find that the rat has eaten the snake – or, at best, seriously savaged it.

If you are really enterprising, a boa constrictor makes an excellent pet. In spite of their popular reputation, these are among the most docile of snakes and can quite quickly be trained to eat their rats, mice and chicks freshly killed. They have perhaps one drawback: they grow at the rate of about 5 ft a year until they attain their adult length of 25 ft. Nevertheless if you are planning to keep a large snake as a pet you should consult a specialist pet shop for advice as to its care in addition to its nutrition. Hilaire Belloc issued a warning:

> I had an aunt in Yucatan
> Who bought a Python from a man
> And kept it for a pet.
> She died, because she never knew
> Those simple little rules and few –
> The Snake is living yet.

Larger animals that live outside the house – ponies and goats, for example, or even the little lamb that Mary had – are often treated as pets, but I shall not discuss their diets here. Information about these bigger creatures is better provided by farming books on animal husbandry.

'All Jock Tamson's Bairns'

There is a Scottish saying that 'we are all Jock Tamson's bairns'. This means that we are all children of Mr Everyman or, to put the thought into biblical language, that all men are brothers. The science of nutrition takes the matter further. In spite of the minor differences that exist between rats and guinea pigs, say, or between birds and beasts, there is an underlying unity in the life process of all living things. In terms of nutrients – calories, protein, vitamins and all the rest – we and our pets need to eat much the same mixture of components to keep our bodies' machinery going. It is only in the selection of the menu that we differ to any marked degree. Partly, this difference is due to differences in equipment for chewing and digesting; partly it is a matter of taste. This being so, it is clear that the principles of nutrition that apply to us apply equally to our pets; eating enough but not too much (nobody loves a fat cat or an obese dog, nor is either of them healthy), and eating a well-varied diet. Choosing what people (and pets) like and are accustomed to is obviously as important for the animals as it is for us. No diet, be it ever so nourishing, is any use if the pet (or the person) for whom it is intended refuses to eat it.

SEVEN

The World Family

'YOU'VE GOT... OYSTER THROAT, CAVIAR TOE, AND STEAK-ON-THE-BRAIN. THAT'LL BE £399!'

'The fundamentals of nutrition are money and knowledge.'

THROUGHOUT THE WORLD we all share the same nutritional needs, even though in different countries we obtain our needs from different kinds of food. Prosperous citizens of industrial countries can, if they like, choose to eat either an expensive and luxurious diet, or an everyday diet drawn from the diversity and variety that the High Street supermarket can supply or a simple back-to-nature diet little different from that eaten in developing countries. The fundamentals of nutrition are *money* and *knowledge*.

Food for Rich and Poor

The true benefit of prosperity, that is, of being rich, is that it confers the freedom to choose. Rich people lacking in knowledge may suffer from malnutrition although the effects of their malnutrition – heart disease, diabetes, perhaps obesity – will be different from those from which poor people suffer and sometimes die. In the main, people with money choose to eat more meat, poultry, fish, cheese, butter and so forth – collectively often called 'animal foods' – than do those for whom money is short. This was first demonstrated back in 1936 in John Boyd Orr's examination of just what British families ate, in which he compared the families of skilled craftsmen with those of lower wage earners. Casual workers and their families, he found, were at the lowest nutritional level of all.

Three important conclusions emerged from Orr's study. The first was that people like meat and, if they can afford to buy it, do so. The second was that those who are least well off are often least knowledgeable about how best to use what little money they have to buy good nutrition. The third conclusion was that really poor people may not have enough money for them to buy their nutritional needs, no matter how skilfully they go shopping. The solution to the problem of poverty can never be complete; but in Great Britain Boyd Orr's message was taken seriously and since his survey all sorts of schemes to improve the nation's nutrition have been introduced. Welfare clinics were established for mothers and babies, milk was provided for infants and schoolchildren and a variety of financial measures developed aimed at ensuring that everyone should have at least enough money to buy the necessary food. The upshot is that in a politically mature country such as Great Britain, even though hardship is experienced by individuals here and there (e.g., the families of low-paid workers and some old people living alone) there is little serious malnutrition and no one is starving.

Since the 1930s, the kind of information Orr collected in Great Britain has been gathered in other countries, and his conclusions have been found to apply worldwide. The people in the richest countries of the world eat the largest proportion of animal foods in their diets, while in progressively poorer countries, the people on average eat less and less meat. In addition, in wealthy countries where the people enjoy plenty of beef, mutton and pork, eggs, milk and cheese, the agriculture is usually modern and efficient. This means that the hens that produce the eggs are often fed on imported grain, and so are the pigs which may also be given milk and meat products as well. High-yielding dairy cows are also given rich feed which is either grown or imported specially for them. Even the sheep graze on land that could be used to grow food that could be eaten directly by people. It can be calculated that the diet of the prosperous industrial nations – containing a high proportion of animal foods and consequently a lower proportion of cereal and vegetable foods – may represent nearly *three times* as much food per person as is eaten in poor unindustrialised countries.

The question is, does it matter? since a mainly vegetarian diet *can* be, as complete and nourishing as a diet containing a large amount of meat. But two things are necessary for this to be so: the first is knowledge and the second is income. At the present time at least, there is no insuperable difficulty in producing enough food to meet the demands of the people of the world. It has proved more difficult, however, to provide everyone with enough money to enable them to buy it.

When times are hard, they are hardest for the citizens of the poorest countries. Where people's diets have plenty of meat in them they can always change to sandwiches, beans on toast, or spaghetti. People who live mainly on rice, however, and who get little meat at any time can do little when times become harder still but tighten their belts. And hardship is most difficult to bear when, as all too often happens, the difference between the way of life of the rich members of the community and that of the poorest may be enormously greater than in a more prosperous and politically mature society.

Who are the Starving Millions?

It is often said that somewhere, far away in some distant tropical country, the people are starving. It is not clear, however, whether as you enter the country *all* the people you see are starving or only some of them; nor do many of those whose sympathies are aroused have any clear idea of what they mean by 'starving'. Certainly, the variety of foods available to the population of a poor nation is less than we are accustomed to, and many people can buy less food than they want to have. Real starvation, however, is mercifully comparatively rare.

Famine, when people starve, may be due to some exceptional natural disaster such as a flood or an earthquake. The appalling famine in Ireland in the 1840s was caused by three exceptionally wet and humid summers that favoured the spread of potato blight, with the consequent destruction of almost the whole of the potato

harvest on which the Irish peasants depended. Throughout history, famines have been caused by war; indeed
famine is used as a military weapon by every nation that can
bring it to bear through sieges and blockades.

Starvation can best be described as the condition in
which people get so little food that they are, as it were,
consuming their own tissues in order to stay alive. People
on short rations will become thin and then remain at a
certain degree of thinness. People who are starving will
become progressively thinner and more emaciated until
they die. (Sometimes they become grossly fat with a dropsy
called 'hunger oedema'. These people, however, are not
overweight in the ordinary sense; they are waterlogged.)
Not long ago it was calculated that approximately 2 per
cent of the world's population could be starving. Although
this amounts to the dreadful total of about 70 million
people, it may well be *proportionately* fewer than ever
before in the world's history.

Where are they? China is a great populous country which is
traditionally subject to the disasters of flood and earthquake, and its history lists many famines. Today, such
information that we have implies that the general nutrition
of the Chinese is satisfactory, not because the country is
rich, but because the administration is efficient and the
social system egalitarian.

In India, too, many people have – and always have had –
little to eat. When the monsoon rains fail, as happens from
time to time, people in the most severely affected areas may
be reduced to desperate straits. During the century of
British rule, great efforts were made to deal with famine in
India. Granaries were built to store the surpluses from
good harvests, and an emergency code was drawn up to
deal with food crisis conditions. (It is still used to guide the
Indian authorities today.) In addition, modern scientific
knowledge has been applied. In 1977 it was reported that
where Indian women had been taught to read and had

received instruction in basic nutrition, the infant death-rate had been reduced by something like 70 per cent.

On the other hand, poverty and a shortage of proper food, perhaps not reaching the harshness of famine but nevertheless representing severe hardship, is still experienced by people in remote and poor areas. *The Grapes of Wrath* was written in 1939, but it cannot be guaranteed that the problems it described have disappeared for all time.

In short, the starving millions are made up of the least fortunate members of any community afflicted by a variety of disasters. The warding off of such calamities requires constant vigilance, appropriate facilities, knowledge and, above all, the social will of a concerned community.

Will the Food Run Out?

People often talk about the 'world food crisis' as though the population of the earth is increasing so fast that quite soon there will not be enough for them all to eat. The facts, however, are different.

The power of science has nowhere been more effectively applied than in food production. Canada, to take one example, is in many respects unsuited to wheat growing: the climate is too dry and the season is too short for most common wheat varieties to thrive there. Even now the yield of wheat per acre is very much greater in England and parts of Europe than in Canada. Yet scientific plant-breeders have developed wheat varieties that can yield immense crops on the Canadian prairies. Each time that a fungus disease has appeared, new resistant varieties have been produced that are unaffected by the attack. The same has been achieved in other parts of the world for rice, maize and other staple foods. And this success with cereals has been repeated for livestock. The yield of milk and the production of meat and eggs have all been greatly increased. Progress in the world's food production since the 1950s has been such that, rapid though the increase in the growth of human numbers has been, the increase in the world's food supply has, till now at least, been greater still.

This does not imply that all has been well for everybody. When Sir John Boyd Orr took up his post as the first Director General of the Food and Agriculture Organization of the United Nations, he was struck by the painful paradox that there were people with too little to eat in Asia at the same time that American farmers were oppressed by a glut of wheat that they could not sell and that some were consequently compelled to burn. In 1977 another bumper harvest, instead of proving a blessing, was the cause of a drastic fall in the price of wheat to the growers. At the same time, careful planners in Europe, anxious to maximise food production, fixed prices at high levels to encourage farmers to grow more, and then found to their distress 'mountains' of butter, meat and dried milk piling up which even wealthy European customers could not afford.

Boyd Orr's paradox still holds: food shortages are not due in the main to the land's inability to produce the crops that the world's population needs but to the people being too poor to buy what agriculture, by making use of science, could produce.

'Not By Bread Alone'

Although nutritional well-being does indeed depend on the diet providing enough to eat and being composed of appropriate proportions of each of the different nutrients the body requires, other matters are equally important to satisfactory nutrition. For instance, prices must be high enough to make it worth the farmers' while to produce the food in the first place and, in most countries, there must be a complex system of transport, storage and processing to make sure that the food that *is* produced gets from the place where it is grown to the people who want to eat it. The food itself must be acceptable to the people for whom it is intended and, finally, the consumers must not only know what kind of food they need for good nutrition but they must also be able to get the right kind of food for health and well-being, either by having the necessary money or by other means. *All* these things – and not only a knowledge of calories, protein and all the rest – are connected with good nutrition the world over.

UNITS

In the main, wherever I have mentioned quantities in this book I have used the units of measurement with which I, and probably you, are most familiar: ounces, calories and so forth. For those who are more at ease with the gram and the kilojoule, I append some useful conversion factors.

$$1 \text{ ounce (oz)} = 28 \text{ grams (g)}$$
$$1 \text{ pound (lb)} = 454 \text{ grams (g)}$$
$$2.2 \text{ pounds (lb)} = 1 \text{ kilogram (kg)}$$

$$1 \text{ fluid ounce (fl oz)} = 28 \text{ millilitres (ml) (or cubic}$$
$$\text{centimetres) (cm}^3)$$
$$1 \text{ pint} = 0.57 \text{ litres (l)}$$
$$1.75 \text{ pints} = 1 \text{ litre (l)}$$

$$0.24 \text{ Calorie (Cal)} = 1 \text{ kilojoule (kJ)}$$
$$1 \text{ Calorie (Cal)} = 4.2 \text{ kilojoules (kJ)}$$
$$1 \text{ Calorie (Cal)} = 1,000 \text{ calories (cal)}$$

INDEX

affluence, sufferings due to, 68
Africa, need for knowledge of
nutrition, 151; coarse diet, 24
agriculture, efficiency in rich
countries, 244; power of science,
247, 248
alcohol, and weight, 33, 50; a food,
49–50; national differences in
consumption, 50; malnutrition
from excesses, 51; and pregnancy,
131–2; teenagers and, 148
allergies, see food allergy
anaemia, commonest nutritional
defect, 16; from alcohol excesses,
51; from menstruation, 57, 62,
63–4; from iron deficiency, 64;
during pregnancy, 130; in the very
old, 171, 172; use of folic acid, 171;
value of black treacle, 172, 201
animals, 221–2; see also pets
appetite, and obesity, 34; upset by
alcoholic excesses, 51; during
convalescence, 86; in teenagers,
145–6
Asia, need for knowledge of
nutrition, 15; food shortages
during US glut, 248
astronauts, calcium loss while lying
down, 86
athletic prowess, unrelated to food
fads, 36; use of glucose, 37; need
for salt, 38
Ayres, Pam, on puddings, 68

babies, 42; rapid growth rate, 91–2,
105, 109; use of cod-liver oil
capsules, 94; survival body stores,
104, 175; value of breast-feeding,
104; special characteristics, 104-5;
getting enough to eat, 105–6, 114;
breast feeding/bottle-feeding
assessments, 106–8; and their
mothers, 107; vitamin needs, 198–9;
bottle-feeding, 110–11; need for
water, 111; and iron, 112, 113;
signs of underfeeding, 114-15;
overfeeding, 115–16; need for
exercise, 116; part of loving family
group, 117, 118–19; choice of food,
117–18; and spinach, 205
beer, commonest cause of obesity,

31–2, 33; salted, 38; harmless in
moderation, 49
beriberi and pellagra, 51; unknown in
rich countries, 13
birds, dietary needs, 232; deficiency
diseases, 232; need for water, 233;
budgerigars, 233; canaries, 233;
mina birds, 234; parrots, 233–4
birth rate (conception), unconnected
with nutrition, 121
blood pressure, increased by salt
consumption 46, 185–6; and
pregnancy, 129, 130; and
overweight, 185
bones, growth of, 81–2; chalk
composition, 81
bowel movement, 23–4
bread, starch component, 21; 'staff of
life', 21–2, 68–70; complements to,
28; addition of salt, 38–9;
white/brown virtues arguments, 45,
99, 197–9; source of protein, 78;
eating cheaply, 158
bread, white, additions to, 15, 63,
81, 148; and availability to zinc, 100;
universal availability, 100;
substitutes, 148–9
breathing, food allergy (hay fever;
asthma), 190

cake, 218–19
calcium, needed by children, 16;
component of bones, 81, 125, 173;
dissolution during prolonged lying
in bed, 86, 173–4; in a milk-free
diet, 94; needed during pregnancy,
125; sources of, 125; loss with
advancing age, 178; needed by
puppies, 223; by water tortoises,
236
Calories, definition, 20;
consumption, 68; children's and
adults' needs, 74–5; and pregnancy,
124
Canada, scientific wheat plant-
breeders, 247
cancer, unrelated to diet, 193–4
carbohydrates, 9, 22–3
cereals, breakfast, 21, 26; liked by
children, 98, 208; cheaper
substitutes, 157; alleged 'junk' food,